U0483727

符号中国 SIGNS OF CHINA

中国姓氏

CHINESE SURNAMES

"符号中国"编写组 ◎ 编著

中央民族大学出版社
China Minzu University Press

图书在版编目(CIP)数据

中国姓氏：汉文、英文 / "符号中国"编写组编著. —北京：
中央民族大学出版社，2024.3
（符号中国）
ISBN 978-7-5660-2291-2

Ⅰ.①中… Ⅱ.①符… Ⅲ.①姓氏—介绍—中国—汉、英 Ⅳ.①K810.2

中国国家版本馆CIP数据核字（2024）第016884号

符号中国：中国姓氏 CHINESE SURNAMES

编　　著	"符号中国"编写组
策划编辑	沙　平
责任编辑	陈　琳
英文指导	李瑞清
英文编辑	邱　械
美术编辑	曹　娜　郑亚超　洪　涛
出版发行	中央民族大学出版社
	北京市海淀区中关村南大街27号　　邮编：100081
	电话：（010）68472815（发行部）　传真：（010）68933757（发行部）
	（010）68932218（总编室）　　　　（010）68932447（办公室）
经 销 者	全国各地新华书店
印 刷 厂	北京兴星伟业印刷有限公司
开　　本	787 mm×1092 mm 1/16　印张：8
字　　数	105千字
版　　次	2024年3月第1版　2024年3月第1次印刷
书　　号	ISBN 978-7-5660-2291-2
定　　价	58.00元

版权所有　侵权必究

"符号中国"丛书编委会

唐兰东　巴哈提　杨国华　孟靖朝　赵秀琴

本册编写者

上官言灵

前 言 Preface

姓氏是被烙在人类身上的文化标志，体现着人类对民族渊源及血脉关系的一种追溯。中国是世界上最早使用姓氏的国家，姓氏使用的历史已有五千多年。中国姓氏经过发展和演变、延续和传承，已经成为一种博大精深的传统文

Surnames are cultural marks imprinted on human beings, which bear traces of racial origins and blood relationships. China has used surnames for more than 5,000 years, the earliest country to have adopted the practice. The way Chinese surnames have developed, changed, continued, and

化，是中华文明的重要标志和中华民族文化库的重要组成部分。中国姓氏不仅是维系民族凝聚力和向心力的纽带，也是海内外中国人寻根问祖的重要依据。

通过本书对中国姓氏的来历、源流，姓氏与寻根，中国常见姓氏等内容的介绍，读者可以更加深入、全面地了解中国的姓氏文化。

progressed represents a profound part of the traditional culture. It is a significant sign of Chinese civilization as well as an important component of the Chinese people and culture. Chinese surnames are not only the cohesive bond and centripetal force of Chinese people, but also the important basis for overseas Chinese descendants to trace their origins.

This book serves to introduce the sources and development of Chinese surnames, and its importance in searching for one's roots. It also explores common surnames, in order to help readers gain a deeper and comprehensive understanding of the culture of Chinese surnames.

目录 Contents

中国姓氏寻根
Searching for the Roots of Chinese Surnames 001

姓氏的来历
Origins of Surnames 002

姓氏的源流
Development of Surnames 017

姓氏与寻根
Surnames and Root-searching 025

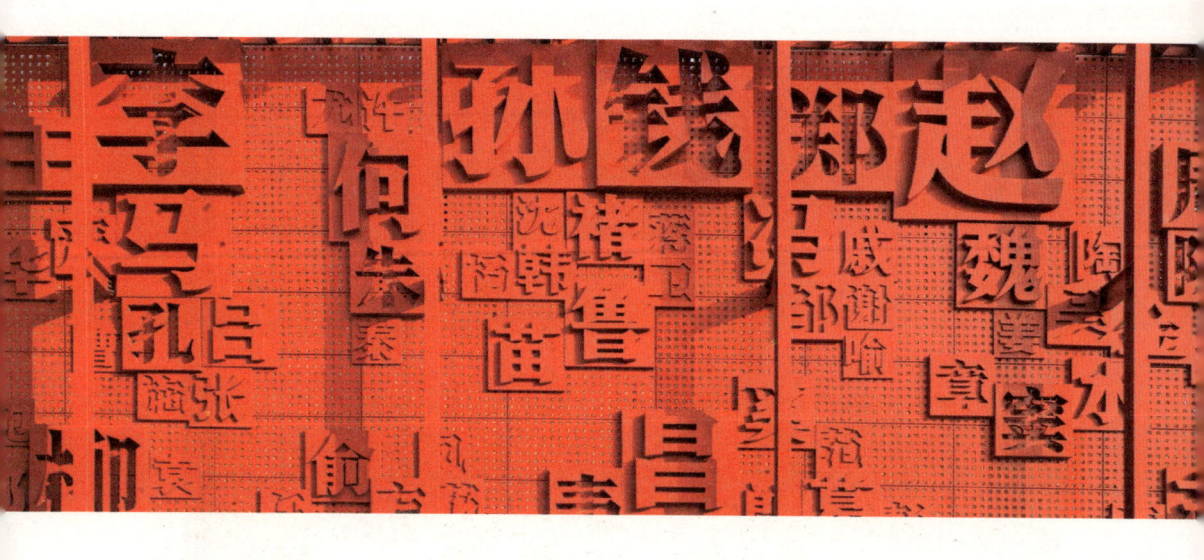

细数中国姓氏
Introducing Chinese Surnames 039

《百家姓》
Book of Hundred Family Names 040

常见姓氏
Common Surnames 047

中国姓氏寻根

Searching for the Roots of Chinese Surnames

　　姓氏作为重要的媒介，能够帮助人们追溯历史、寻根过去。中国人以共同祖先的姓氏作为血脉传承纽带的文化传统，构成了中华民族的凝聚力。

As an important medium, surnames can help people trace their history, and discover their roots. The cultural tradition that the basis of Chinese surnames derive from the same ancestors creates a bond between all Chinese people.

> 姓氏的来历

中国姓氏是中华文化体系的重要组成部分。在氏族社会，姓、氏先后产生；在夏商周时期，姓、氏在分封制度的影响下得以发展；在秦汉时期，姓、氏统一，合并为"姓氏"。

据传，姓氏起源于图腾崇拜。上古时期，原始人相信自然界万物有灵，对图腾的崇拜产生。他们将某种动物、植物等当作本部族的"保护神"来祭祀，还将它们作为部落特有的徽号或标志，后来逐渐演变成了最古老的姓氏。

相传，夏族首领禹的母亲因吞食薏苡而生下了他。从此，薏苡便成为夏族人的图腾。因为孩子是由女性生育的，便取"女"字作为偏旁，又取"苡"字的下半部分"以"字，最终

> Origins of Surnames

Chinese surnames is an important part of Chinese cultural system. In the clan society, surnames *(Xing)* and clan names *(Shi)* came into being successively. In the Xia, Shang and Zhou dynasties, surnames and clan names developed under the feudal system of enfeoffment. During the Qin and Han dynasties, surnames and clan names became one under the general term of surname *(Xingshi)*.

It is generally held that surnames originated from totemism. In ancient times, people's belief in animism contributed to worship of totems. Certain animals and plants were worshipped and offered sacrifices as the guardian deities of their clans. They were also referred to in the emblems or symbols of their tribes which, later, gradually became the oldest surnames.

形成了"姒"姓。

《史记》中也有类似的记载："殷契，母曰简狄，有娀氏之女，为帝喾次妃。三人行浴，见玄鸟堕其卵，简狄取吞之，因孕生契。"契是商族的祖先，他的母亲因为吞食玄鸟产的卵而生下了他。由此，玄鸟便成为商族的图腾，商族人以"子"（即"卵"）为姓。

• 大禹像
Portrait of Yu the Great

The legend has it that the mother of Yu, head of the Tribe Xia, gobbled a plant called Job's tears (a Poales plant) and then gave birth to Yu. Thereafter, Job's tears became the totem of the Tribe Xia. Since children were given birth by females, the Chinese character "女"(female, *Nü*) was adopted to replace the original upper part of the character of "苡" (Job's tears, *Yi*), the surname of "姒" (*Si*) was henceforth formed.

Similar tales can also be found in the *Historical Records*, "Jian Di, Yin Xie's mother and daughter of the clan of You Song, was the second wife to Emperor Ku. While bathing, Jian Di saw a Xuan Bird (a legendary bird) laying an egg. She ate the egg and was pregnant with Yin Xie." Yin Xie was the ancestor of the Tribe Shang. Since his mother born him after eating Xuan Bird's egg, the bird became the totem of the Tribe Shang and the character *Zi* (meaning egg) was used as the surname of the tribe.

Surnames made their first appearance during the times of matriarchal society when people "only knew their mothers instead of fathers". Men and women both inherited their surnames from female ancestors. Surnames were originally used as characters to mark the family and clan

名、字、号
Given Names, Courtesy Names and Title Names

名

在姓氏还没有产生的时候，古人使用的是名。名是一个人的标志性符号，即一个人的代称。名起源于氏族社会，常与姓连用。儒学经典《周礼》中记载："婚生三月而加名。"

Given Names

As an identifiable symbol for a person, the given name originated in clan society and has been a personal indicator used in combination with the surname. Ancient people used given names before surnames came into being. In the Confucian classic *Rites of Zhou*, it is recorded that, "A born-in-wedlock baby is to be given a name at the third month after birth."

字

字又称"表"，是名之外古人的又一称呼。南北朝时期的文学家颜之推（531—约595）在其著作《颜氏家训》中写道："古者，名以正体，字以表德"。字是与名相关联的一个称谓，即"别名"，多用来表示一个人的品德。古人一般都有名和字，男子一般在二十岁行冠礼（男子的成年礼）时取字，女子一般在十五岁行笄礼（女子成年礼）时取字。古人在自称的时候用名；在称呼他人的时候则用字，以表尊敬。如今，取字的习俗已不多见。

Courtesy Names

The courtesy name, also known as the style name, was used in addition to the given name by ancient people. Yan Zhitui (531-c.595), a literary writer of the Southern and Northern dynasties (420-589), wrote in his *Admonitions of the Yan Clan* that, "In ancient times, given names were used to identify a person while courtesy names were meant to declare a person's virtues." A courtesy name is related to the given name of a person; it's an alternative given name used to indicate a person's virtues. People in the ancient times used to have both the given name and the courtesy name. Courtesy names were given when boys attended the crowning ceremony (the come-of-age ceremony for boys) at the age of 20 and girls joined the hair-pinning ceremony (the come-of-age ceremony for girls) at 15. People in ancient times usually used given names when referring to themselves and used courtesy names when referring to others as a gesture of respect. Nowadays, courtesy names are rarely used.

号

号是古人名、字之外的别称。据记载，号在春秋时期就已出现。相对于名和字，号的选取要自由得多，不必受家族、辈分、制度等方面的影响，根据每个人的不同喜好而选取。

Title Names

The title name is an alternative that ancient people used in addition to the given name and the courtesy name. According to records, title names were already used in the Spring and Autumn Period (770 B.C.-476 B.C.). In contrast to given names and courtesy names, title names were chosen without influence from family background, family hierarchy, social systems and the like. Everyone could choose the title name to one's own liking.

- 玄鸟

出自《山海经》，即黑色的燕子。

Xuan Bird

Originally seen in the *Classic of Mountains and Seas*, the Xuan Bird is a black swallow.

姓最早出现在母系氏族社会时期。这一时期，人们"只知其母，不知其父"，人们的姓是从女性始祖那里继承来的，无论男女，都有姓。姓的本义为标志着家族系统的 systems. It stood for the common blood relationship for descendants. According to the definition in *Explaining and Analyzing Characters* by Xu Shen, a philologist of the Eastern Han Dynasty (25-220), "*Xing* ('姓' in Chinese, meaning surname) means the birth of a human. In ancient times, *Xing* denoted a heavenly-impregnated mother giving birth to a child, hence the term 'son of heaven'. The character is composed of '女' (*Nü*, female) and '生' (*Sheng*, give birth to), a homonym of *Sheng* (the sound)." The definition shows that surnames were originated from mothers; therefore, surnames in the ancient times, such as "姜" (*Jiang*), "姬" (*Ji*), "姒" (*Si*), "嬴"

- **女娲补天**

相传，古时候天露了一个洞，导致地上火灾、洪水不断，猛兽也经常出没伤人，民不聊生。于是女娲炼五色石头以补天，最终解救了地上的百姓。

Nüwa Mending Firmament

As the legend goes, there was a time in remote antiquity that a hole in the sky gave rise to fires and incessant flooding on earth, and people were being hurt frequently by animals. Seeing people losing their means of livelihood, Nüwa used stones of five colors to mend the hole in the sky and eventually saved all the common people on earth.

字，代表着子孙后代的共同血缘。东汉时期的文字学家许慎在他撰写的《说文解字》中对"姓"进行了注释："姓，人所生也。古之神圣，母感天而生子，故称天子。从女从生，生亦声。"这是说，姓源

(Ying), "姞" (Ji), "妘" (Yun) and the like, were all composed of the Chinese radical "女" (Nü, female). From the very beginning, surnames have been used as marks to prevent same-surname marriages. *White Tiger Hall Annotations*, a classic from the Han Dynasty (206 B.C.-220 A.D.) to reconcile scholastic contradictions, explains: the reason why people have surnames is that surnames can promote affection, emphasize blood relationships, differentiate people from animals, and prevent same-surname marriage. During the periods of primitive society, it was recognized that "people with the same surname came from the same family root". Same-surname marriage was against ethical codes, and might beget deformed births. Therefore, a taboo arose to forbid marriage between people bearing the same surname.

The clan name first appeared in patriarchal society times. During this period, men had displaced women as leaders. Clan names were inherited from patriarchs and only males were entitled to clan names. Due to the rise of the hierarchical system, in clans where people use the same surnames, differences in wealth and class came about and further divisions of clans branched out on the

伏羲、女娲

相传，伏羲和女娲为人首蛇身的"神"，他们既是兄妹，也是夫妻。皇甫谧的史书著作《帝王世纪》中记载："太昊帝庖牺氏，风姓也。"伏羲与女娲因生于风沟而姓"风"，是中国最早使用"风"姓的人。

宋代典籍《太平御览》记载："伏羲坐于方坛之上，听八风之气，乃画八卦。"八卦是伏羲为观察自然万物而发明的。除此之外，伏羲教先民结网捕鱼，投矛狩猎，用兽皮缝制衣服，并与女娲一起开创了最早的婚姻制度。西汉典籍《淮南子》中记载了女娲炼五色石以补苍天的神话传说。

Fuxi and Nüwa

Legend has it that Fuxi and Nüwa were gods with human heads and snake bodies. They were both siblings and spouses. As shown in *Records of Emperors and Kings* by Huangfu Mi:"Fuxi was surnamed Feng (wind)." Fuxi and Nüwa were surnamed Feng since they were born at Fenggou (lit. Ditch of Wind). They were the first to use the surname Feng in China.

- **甲骨文"风"**

甲骨文是在殷商时期出现的一种具有较为严密的系统的文字，已有3000多年的历史，是中国目前已知的最早的文字。这些文字被刻在龟甲、兽骨上，因此得名"甲骨文"。

Character of "风" (*Feng*, Wind) in Oracle Bone Script

As the earliest known written language in China dating back to around 3,000 years ago, the oracle bone script was a comparatively systemized writing system which appeared in the Shang Dynasty (1600 B.C.-1046 B.C.). These written languages were inscribed on tortoise shells and animal bones for oracle purposes, and were thus known as the oracle bone script.

The *Imperial Readings of the Taiping Era* of the Song Dynasty (960-1279) recorded that, "Fuxi sat on a square platform, listened to the wind from eight directions, and drew the Eight Diagrams." The Eight Diagrams were invented by Fuxi through his observation of numerous beings in nature. In addition, Fuxi also taught ancient people how to make fishing nets, use spears to hunt, and make clothing out of furs. Fuxi and Nüwa also created the earliest marriage system. The myth in *Huai Nan Zi* (lit. *The Masters/Philosophers of Huainan*) of the Western Han Dynasty (206 B.C.-25 A.D.) also recorded that Nüwa used stones of five colors to mend the damaged firmament.

- **伏羲创八卦图**

八卦以"—"为阳，以"--"为阴，依次为乾、坤、震、巽、坎、艮、离、兑，分别与自然界的天、地、雷、风、水、山、火、泽对应。古时，人们用八卦进行占卜。

Fuxi Creating the Eight Diagrams

The Eight Diagrams are built up on two constituent symbols: the straight horizontal line "—" stands for *Yang* and the broken horizontal line " -- " represents *Yin*. The Eight Diagrams are *Qian, Kun, Zhen, Xun, Kan, Gen, Li* and *Dui*, representing respectively the eight phenomenons of heaven, earth, thunder, wind, water, mountain, fire and lake in nature. In ancient times, people used the Eight Diagrams for divination.

伏羲女娲图（唐）
Picture of Fuxi and Nüwa (Tang Dynasty, 618-907)

自孕育并产子的母亲，因此上古时期的姓，例如姜、姬、姒、嬴、姞、妘等都以"女"字为偏旁。姓从出现开始，就被人们当作"别婚姻"的标志。汉代典籍《白虎通义》中有相关记载："人所以有姓者何？所以崇恩爱，厚亲亲，远禽兽，别

basis of the original consanguinity. These new branches moved out of original gathering places and scattered in different areas. They began to use different clan names. In ancient times, people used clan names to distinguish between high and low status in identity, positions, virtues and achievements, skills and competences and so forth. In *White Tiger Hall Annotations: Chapter of Names*, it says, "Why are there clan names? The clan name is used to indicate virtues and skills." Generally speaking, both nobles and ordinary people could use clan names, though some clan names were exclusively used by certain nobility. Despite the fact that some ordinary people did have clan names, they were still low-classed in comparison with nobles with high virtues and great achievements, for instance, those surnamed Tu (butchering) who took animal-butchering as their profession.

Since the beginning of the patriarchal period, a system that surnames and clan

婚姻也。"因为在原始社会时期，人们认为"同姓是一家"，同姓结婚违背伦理和道德。当时的人们还认识到同姓男女繁育的后代常出现畸形，于是产生了"同姓不婚"的禁忌。

氏最早出现在父系氏族社会时期。这一时期，男性取代女性占据了主导地位。氏是从父系始祖那里继承来的，且只有男子才称"氏"。阶级制度的产生使同姓宗族中出现了贫富差距和等级分化，在原有的血缘关系的基础上出现了不同的分支。这些分支从原有的聚集地迁出后，分布在不同的地域，用不同的氏来命名。古人用氏来区别身份、地位、功德、伎力等的高低，《白虎通义·姓名》中记载："所以有氏者何？所以贵功德，贱伎力。"一般而言，贵族、平民都可以用氏，只是有一些氏为贵族所专有。平民即使有氏，相对于功高德重的贵族也较为低贱，例如以屠宰牲畜为职业的屠氏等。

从父系氏族社会时期开始，姓与氏并行的双轨制度得以确立。在夏商周时期，姓氏双轨制度仍

names were both used was established. In the Xia, Shang and Zhou dynasties, this system continued to be used. For example, the monarchs of the Xia Dynasty had the surname of Si and the clan name of Xia: Shang monarchs had Zi for the surname and Shang for the clan name: while the Zhou monarchs had Ji and Zhou respectively for their surname and clan name.

The Xia Dynasty was a society where the slavery system was established. Due to a man's higher status and functions, coupled with the influence of the expanded range of human activities, surnames and the matriarchal system of blood relations they stood for gradually fell apart, losing their practical function of preventing same-surname marriage while clan names gradually developed on the basis of the patriarchal clan system. The government of Zhou implemented the enfeoffment system during the Western Zhou Dynasty (1046 B.C.-771 B.C.) with land conferred and clan names dubbed for the purpose of solidifying the political power of the state. In the enfeoffment system, vassalage was awarded to imperial kinsmen, to officials with acknowledged achievements and to leaders of ancient tribes so that they

然延续。例如夏代国君以"姒"为姓，以"夏"为氏；商代国君以"子"为姓，以"商"为氏；周代国君以"姬"为姓，以"周"为氏。

夏代时，奴隶制社会被建立，并逐步完善，男性的地位远远高于女性，作用远远大于女性。且受人类活动范围扩大的影响，姓代表的

- **龙凤纹瓷器（清）**
龙、凤图腾是中华民族最为古老的图腾符号。传说龙图腾由黄帝创造，凤图腾则由黄帝的妻子嫘祖创造。龙、凤在中国人心中是吉祥的象征。

Chinaware of Dragon and Phoenix (Qing Dynasty,1616-1911)
Dragons and phoenixes are the oldest totem of Chinese people. Legend has it that the totem of dragon was created by Huangdi while the totem of phoenix was created by his wife Leizu. Dragon and phoenix are symbols of auspice in Chinese culture.

could build up their vassal states in various areas. Based on the location of their vassal states, they were conferred with clan names which could be passed down to their heirs. While the branches belonging to the same clan increased, the amount of clan names also multiplied accordingly during this period. In addition to using the names of vassal states or places as clan names, ancient people also used official titles, posthumous titles (titles conferred on rulers or high-status people after they died), and professions of their ancestors and others as clan names.

During the Spring and Autumn Period and Warring States Period, the national power of imperial court of Zhou waned while feudal lords were dividing and seizing the land for their own interests in competition for hegemony. The original enfeoffment system collapsed and clan names, which represented one's status and identity, gradually lost its original function. The difference between surnames and clan names became blurred. They eventually became synonyms. Prior to this, the difference between surnames and clan names served mainly three purposes: (1) to differentiate the exclusive usage

母系血缘系统逐渐趋于瓦解，不再具有"别婚姻"的实际作用，氏则在宗法制的基础上逐渐发展起来。西周时期，周王朝实行分封制，"胙之土而命之氏"，以巩固国家政权。分封制就是将同姓的王族、有功之臣、先代的部落首领等分封到各地去做诸侯，建立诸侯国，并根据其所在地赐予他们"氏"，这个代表家族的氏是可以继承的。同氏的分支不断增多，使得这一时期

of clan names by males and surnames by females; (2) to distinguish between the high and low classes; (3) to provide a guidance for marriage. People with the same clan names and different surnames could marry while marriage between people with same surnames but different clan names should be avoided.

During the Qin and Han dynasties, the unified feudal state replaced the slave society. With imperial and noble privileges as well as the original

- **宜侯夨（cè）簋复制品（西周）** （图片提供：FOTOE）

簋是一种盛食器，此宜侯夨簋上刻有铭文120多字，记载了周康王册封夨为宜侯的历史。此铭文是关于西周分封制的重要史料。

The Replica of Yihou *Ce Gui* (Western Zhou Dynasty, 1046 B.C.-771 B.C.)

Gui is a food container. The Yihou *Ce Gui* was inscribed more than 120 epigraphs. The record was probably Zhou Kang Wang canonized Ce for Yihou. The epigraph was important historical materials that the government of Zhou implemented the enfeoffment system during the Western Zhou Dynasty.

宗法制

宗法制是中国古代实行的一种世袭制度，由氏族社会父系家长制演变而来，最早出现在夏代，周代时得以完备。周代实行严格的等级制度，从高至低依次为天子、诸侯、卿大夫、士、平民和奴隶。古时实行"一夫多妻"制，正妻生的儿子为嫡子，其他侧室生的儿子为庶子，只有嫡长子（正妻生的第一个儿子）才拥有王位、爵位或官职的继承权。

Patriarchal Clan System

The patriarchal clan system was a hereditary system implemented in ancient China. It was first seen in the Xia Dynasty and perfected in the Zhou Dynasty. In the Zhou Dynasty (1046 B.C.-256 B.C.), the hierarchal system was rigorously implemented from the highest position of the emperor through feudal vassals, ministers, scholars, common people down to the lowest slaves. According to the polygynous system in ancient times, those sons born by the first wife were called *Dizi* (sons born of the legal wife of a man) while those by the concubines were the called *Shuzi* (concubine's children). Only the eldest *Dizi* (the first son of the first wife) was entitled to inherit the throne, the title, the official post or the property of the father.

- 甲骨文拓片（商代）（图片提供：FOTOE）
  此甲骨文大意为：是否需要以女奴隶为祭品来祭祀河神？
  The Oracle Bone Rubbing (Shang Dynasty, 1600 B.C.-1046 B.C.)
  The oracle's general meaning was: whether people needed to sacrifice a female slave to the river god?

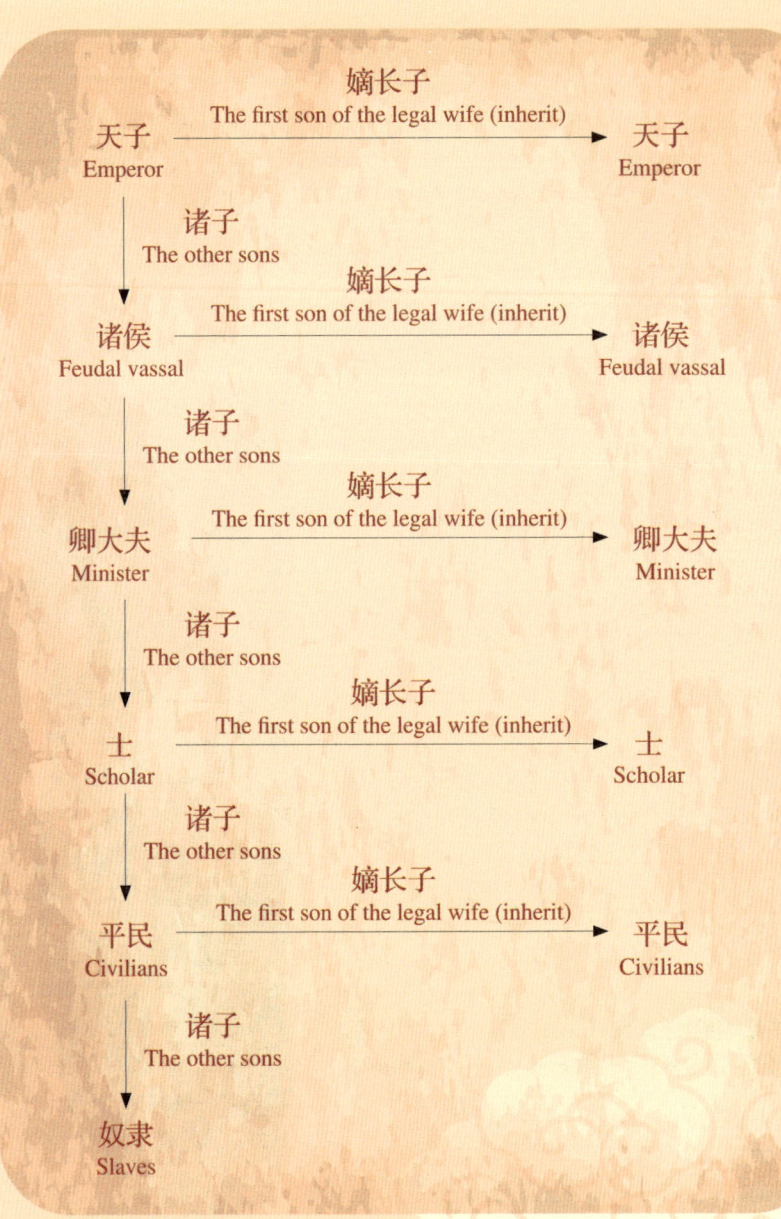

天子 —— 嫡长子 The first son of the legal wife (inherit) ——→ 天子
Emperor　　　　　　　　　　　　　　　　　　　　　　　　　　　　Emperor

↓ 诸子 The other sons

诸侯 —— 嫡长子 The first son of the legal wife (inherit) ——→ 诸侯
Feudal vassal　　　　　　　　　　　　　　　　　　　　　　　　Feudal vassal

↓ 诸子 The other sons

卿大夫 —— 嫡长子 The first son of the legal wife (inherit) ——→ 卿大夫
Minister　　　　　　　　　　　　　　　　　　　　　　　　　　　Minister

↓ 诸子 The other sons

士 —— 嫡长子 The first son of the legal wife (inherit) ——→ 士
Scholar　　　　　　　　　　　　　　　　　　　　　　　　　　　Scholar

↓ 诸子 The other sons

平民 —— 嫡长子 The first son of the legal wife (inherit) ——→ 平民
Civilians　　　　　　　　　　　　　　　　　　　　　　　　　　Civilians

↓ 诸子 The other sons

奴隶
Slaves

- 宗法制继承权演示图
  Diagram of Right of Inheritance in Patriarchal Clan System

氏的数量也随之增加。除了以国家、地名为氏，古人还常常以祖先的官职、谥号（统治者或有地位的人死后，后人追授的称号）、职业等为氏。

春秋战国时期，周王朝国力衰微，各诸侯割据土地、争夺霸权，原有的分封制土崩瓦解，原来代表地位高低、身份贵贱的氏逐渐失去了它的作用。姓与氏的界限逐渐模糊，开始被通用。在此之前，姓与氏被严格区分开来的作用主要体现在三个方面：一是氏和姓分别为男、女所用；二是为了区别阶级的

patriarchal clan system being overthrown, clan names with implications of social status were completely deprived of the function of distinguishing the high and low in class. It bore no significant difference from the surname of consanguinity. With the growing population, the surnames and clan names spread to a broader area, which led to the collapse of the taboo that marriage is forbidden between those with same surnames. In the *Historical Records*, the descriptions of the First Emperor of the Qin Dynasty having the clan name of Zhao as the surname and Emperor

- 司马迁著《史记》
  Sima Qian Compiled *Historical Records*

贵贱；三是为了更好地选择婚姻，同氏不同姓的人可以结婚，同姓不同氏的人则不可以结婚。

秦汉时期，统一的封建制国家取代了奴隶制国家，代表着社会地位的氏也失去了"别贵贱"的作用，与标志着家族血缘关系的姓差别不大。且随着人类的繁衍生息，姓氏的地域性逐渐扩大，"同姓不婚"的禁忌也被打破。司马迁在其著作《史记》中称秦始皇"姓赵氏"，汉高祖"姓刘氏"，标志着姓与氏开始并用，或者兼称"姓氏"，合二为一的姓氏制度得以确立。姓与氏的统一使得中国姓氏的数量和文化内涵得到了极大的丰富。

Gaozu of the Han Dynasty having the clan name of Liu as the surname have already evidenced that surnames and clan names were combined in use. They were generally called surnames, marking the integration of surnames and clan names as a system. The integration of surnames and clan names has thus enriched the number and cultural significance of Chinese surnames.

> ## 姓氏的源流

《国语》中记载："凡黄帝之子二十五宗，其得姓者十四人，为十二姓。"三国时期史学家韦昭注解道："得姓，以德居官，而初赐之姓。谓十四人，而内二人为姬，二人为己，故十二姓。"传说中中国人的始祖黄帝共生有二十五个儿子，他赐予其中十四个人姓，分别为姬、酉、祁、己、滕、箴、任、荀、僖、姞、儇、依，其中有两个人同为姬姓，两个人同为己姓。到秦代为止，黄帝直系子族共分衍出510个姓氏。如今，纷繁复杂的中国姓氏大多是从上古时期的古老姓氏发展而来的。

东汉文学家王符所著的《潜夫论·志氏姓》中记载了中国姓氏的演变方式："或传本姓，或氏号邑

> ## Development of Surnames

It is recorded in *Discourses of the States* that, "Huangdi had 25 sons as descendants, among them 14 inherited and shared the 12 surnames." According to the annotation made by Wei Zhao, a historian from the Three Kingdoms Period (220-280), "The conferment of the surnames was based on virtues. Fourteen sons shared the 12 surnames because two of them had the same surname of Ji (姬) while another two shared Ji (己)." Huangdi, the great ancestor of Chinese people in legend, begot 25 sons, 14 of whom carried over the surnames of Ji (姬), You, Qi, Ji (己), Teng, Zhen, Ren, Xun, Xi, Ji (姞), Xuan and Yi. Up until the Qin Dynasty (221 B.C.-206 B.C.), 510 surnames came from the sub-tribes from the direct lineage of Huangdi. Currently, most of the surnames from this massive and complicated directory

谥，……或氏于爵，……或氏于志"。根据研究结果，姓氏从古至今的演变归纳起来主要有十三种源流：

第一种，以祖先崇拜的图腾为姓氏。前文所讲的有关夏族和商族的姓，都是从氏族部落的图腾逐渐演变的。

● 刻纹青铜礼器拓片（战国）（图片提供：FOTOE）

此刻纹青铜礼器1978年于江苏淮阴高庄战国墓出土，其上刻有与上古巫术有关的山林、禽兽、巫师、怪异神兽等形象的纹饰。

Rubbing of Patterned Bronze Ritual Vessel (Warring States Period, 475 B.C.-221 B.C.)

This patterned bronze ritual vessel was unearthed in 1978 from a tomb of the Warring States Period at the location of Gaozhuang in Huaiyin City, Jiangsu Province. The vessel is adorned with witchcraft-related patterns of mountains and forests, birds and beasts, wizards, as well as extraordinary beasts and divine animals.

of Chinese surnames developed from the ancient surnames before the Xia Dynasty.

Wang Fu, a literary writer from the Eastern Han Dynasty, recorded the development of Chinese surnames in his *Comments of a Recluse*: *Discourse on Surnames*, "It might be handed down from the original surname; or from the clan names, title names and vassal names; or from the feudal title bestowed; or from the ideal harbored." According to research results, the development and transformation of surnames since ancient times may be classified into the following 13 ways:

1. Surnames came from the totems worshiped by the ancestors. The aforementioned surnames of the Tribe Xia and Tribe Shang were derived from the totem names of the clans and tribes.

2. Surnames came from the names, courtesy names and posthumous titles of ancestors. Take the instance of Zhu which came from the name of the ancestor for example. There were four branches of descendants from Dan Zhu, son of Yao (one of the five legendary chiefs during remote antiquity), one of whom took the name Zhu from the forefather as the

柏高

柏高也叫"伯高""柏子高",传说为远古时的巫师。

Bo Gao

Bo Gao, also known as Bo Gao or Bo Zigao, was said to be a wizard from the remote antiquity.

第二种,以祖先的名、字、庙号、谥号为姓氏。例如以祖先的名为姓的朱姓:尧的儿子丹朱的后裔分为四支,其中一支取丹朱名字中的"朱"字为姓。又如以祖先的字为姓的施姓:春秋时期,鲁惠公的

surname. Take another example of the surname Shi. It was derived from the courtesy name of their ancestor, a son of Duke Hui of Lu in the Spring and Autumn Period by the name of Weisheng with the courtesy name of Shifu. His descendants in later generations adopted Shi from his courtesy name as their surname in order to commemorate him.

3. Surnames came from the name of the tribe, the title of the feudal land, or the title of the state. For example, the surname Wei came from the name of a feudal land. In the Western Zhou Dynasty, as the descendant of King Wen of Zhou, Bi Wan was given the feudal land of Wei, their descendants used the name of the feudal land of Wei as their surname. The surname of Jiang came from a state name. During the Western Zhou Period, Duke Wen of Zhou's son, Bo Ling, was given the land of Jiang, where the State of Jiang was established. During the Spring and Autumn Period, the State of Jiang was so small and weak that it was eliminated by the State of Chu. In order to commemorate the home country, its descendants took the name of the State Jiang as their surname.

4. Surnames came from the ancestor's official position or title of

儿子尾生，字施父，其后世子孙为了纪念他，便以其字为姓。

第三种，以部落名、封地名、国名为姓氏。例如以封地名为姓的魏姓：西周时期，周文王的后裔毕万被赐封魏地，其后世子孙便以封地名为姓，称魏氏。以国名为姓的蒋姓：西周时期，周文公的儿子伯龄被封在蒋地，建立了蒋国。春秋时期，蒋国弱小，为楚国所灭，其子孙为了纪念故国，便以国名为姓。

第四种，以先人的爵位、官职为姓氏。例如以官职名为姓的曹姓：舜帝时期，安辅佐夏禹治水有功而被赐曹官，后来他便以官为姓。

第五种，以职业技艺为姓氏。例如卜姓：上古时期，巫术盛行，凡事都要进行占卜，于是有了巫师，他们的子孙后代便以祖先的职业为姓。

第六种，以山河名、地名为姓氏。例如以出生地为姓的姚姓：舜出生在姚虚（今河南濮阳），便以地名姚为姓。之后，一部分族人迁至妫水边（山西境内），便以河名为姓，改为妫

nobility. For example, the surname of Cao came from an official title. During the reign of Emperor Shun, An was awarded with the official position called Cao due to his achievement in helping Yu the Great solve flooding problems. Later, he adopted his official title Cao as the surname.

5. Surnames came from the craftsmanship and profession. For example, the surname of Bu arose from ancient times when witchcraft prevailed so much so that everything had to be consulted with divination (*Bu*). Therefore, wizards appeared and their descendants used their ancestor's profession as their surname.

6. Surnames came from the name of rivers or areas. For instance, Yao was taken for Shun's surname according to his birthplace at Yaoxu (Puyang, in Henan Province). Later, a part of the tribe relocated to the bank of River Gui (in Shanxi Province) and therefore changed their surname to Gui, while those who remained at Yaoxu still kept their original surname of Yao.

7. Surnames came from the location of residence. For example, the surname of Ximen (lit.western gate) came from a minister of the State of Zheng in the

姓；选择留在姚虚的那部分子孙则延续其原有的姚姓。

第七种，以居住地为姓氏。例如西门姓：春秋时期，郑国的一个卿大夫住在都城（今河南新郑）的西门，其子孙后代便以住地的方位为姓。

第八种，以出生时的异象为姓氏。例如武姓：据说，周平王出生时手心有一个篆文"武"字，于是他便以"武"为姓。

- 篆文"武"

篆文是大篆、小篆的统称。大篆包括先秦时期的甲骨文、金文、籀文、六国文字。小篆指秦代通用文字，与大篆相比更加简便。

Character of *Wu* in Seal Script

The seal script is a general term for the large and small seal scripts. And the big seal script includes the oracle bone inscription, bronze inscription, Zhou script, the scripts of the six states in the pre-Qin Period (approx. 2070 B.C.-221 B.C.). And the small seal script was generally used in the Qin Dynasty, which was more convenient and simpler than the big seal script.

Spring and Autumn Period who lived at the western gate of the imperial city. Later, his descendants used the location of the residence Ximen as their surname.

8. Surnames might come from a supernatural phenomenon at birth. Take Wu (lit.martial) for example: It is said that, King Ping of Zhou who was born with the palm print of character of *Wu* in seal script, hence the surname of Wu.

9. Surnames might be changed in order to avoid the taboo of referring the name of emperors or kings, to evade animosity, to escape disaster, to avoid suspicion, and so on. Take Yan for example. When Liu Zhuang, known in history as Emperor Ming of the Han Dynasty, ascended to the throne in the beginning of the Eastern Han Dynasty, people of the Zhuang clan changed their surname to Yan in order to avoid the taboo of referring the name of emperor.

10. Surnames came from virtues. Take the surname of Che (lit.wagon) for example. At the beginning of Western Han Dynasty, Emperor Wu of Han's minion, Jiang Chong, tried to frame Prince Liu Ju by accusing him of conducting witchcraft to curse the emperor. Liu Ju rose to rebel, but failed and escaped. A person by the name of

第九种，因避忌帝王的名讳、避仇、避祸、避嫌等更改姓氏。例如严姓：东汉初期，刘庄继位，史称"汉明帝"，为了避忌他的名讳，庄姓族人改姓严。

第十种，以德行为姓氏。例如车姓：西汉初期，汉武帝的宠臣江充陷害太子刘据，说刘据用巫蛊之术诅咒汉武帝，刘据愤而反抗，失败逃走。一个叫田千秋的人敢于上书进谏，为太子申冤，因此被汉武帝重用，几个月后被封为宰相。汉武帝死后，田千秋仍居丞相之位辅

Tian Qianqiu bravely uttered words of remonstration to redress the injustice on behalf of the prince. Tian was therefore entrusted by the emperor with an important position and promoted to the post of prime minister several months later. After Emperor Wu died, Tian remained in the same office to assist the new emperor in governing the country. Due to his decrepitude, Tian was given the privilege to take a small wagon to enter the palace. He was therefore nicknamed the Wagon Minister and his descendants used Che as their surname.

11. Some surnames were bestowed by emperors. Take Zheng He, the well-known navigator of the Ming Dynasty (1368-1644) for example. His original name was Ma Sanbao, with original birthplace registered at Yunnan. He was captured when he was young and sent to the palace to become an eunuch. In 1399,

• 北魏孝文帝塑像（图片提供：FOTOE）
Sculpture of Emperor Xiaowen of the Northern Wei Dynasty (386-534)

佐新帝，且因年事已高特被恩准可乘小车进入皇宫，于是被称为"车丞相"，其后代子孙便以"车"为姓。

第十一种，帝王赐姓。例如郑姓：明代著名航海家郑和，原名马三保，原籍云南，少时为明军所俘，进入皇宫做宦官。1399年，明太祖朱元璋第四子朱棣发动政变，抢夺了政权，登基称帝。马三保因在此期间立下战功，而被明成祖朱棣赐姓"郑"。

第十二种，以数量词、排行次序、天干、地支为姓氏。例如以排

Zhu Di, the fourth son of Emperor Taizu of Ming (Zhu Yuanzhang), launched a coup, took the throne and became enthroned. Since Ma Sanbao contributed to Zhu Di's achievements during the conflict, Zhu Di, Emperor Chengzu of Ming, bestowed him with the surname of Zheng.

12. Quantifiers, seniority among brothers and sisters, and the calendar terms for heavenly stems and earthly branches were also adopted as surnames. For example, the surname of Ji came from the sibling order. Ji Zha was a noted statesman and diplomat in the Spring and Autumn Period. He was the fourth child in the family. In ancient times, the first brother in the order was called Bo, the second Zhong, the third Shu, and the fourth Ji. In order to commemorate Ji Zha, his descendants used his sibling order Ji as their surname.

- 彩绘披裘男陶俑（北魏）（图片提供：FOTOE）
Color-painted Terracotta of Fur-coated Male (Northern Wei Dynasty, 386-534)

行次序为姓的季姓:季札是春秋时期著名的政治家、外交家,他在家中排行老四。古时兄弟的排行老大称"伯",老二称"仲",老三称"叔",老四称"季"。季札的子孙后代为了纪念他,便以其排行为姓。

第十三种,少数民族汉化改姓。例如元姓:南北朝时期,北魏孝文帝深受汉族文化影响,大力推行政治改革,即"孝文汉化",其中就有鲜卑族改其民族姓氏为汉姓的规定。孝文帝带头将自己的皇族姓氏"拓跋"改为"元",即第一、首个的意思。

13. People of ethnic groups converted their names to Chinese names. Take the surname of Yuan for example. During the Southern and Northern dynasties, Emperor Xiaowen of the Northern Wei Dynasty was so deeply influenced by Chinese culture that he was devoted to the implementation of political reform, known as the Xiaowen's Chinesization. One of the ordinances he issued was to change the ethnic surnames of the Xianbei Tribe into Chinese ones. Emperor Xiaowen took the lead and changed his original imperial surname from Tuoba to Yuan (lit. first or chief).

天干和地支

天干和地支是中国古代干支纪年法中的基本单位。天干分别为甲、乙、丙、丁、戊、己、庚、辛、壬、癸,共十个。地支分别为子、丑、寅、卯、辰、巳、午、未、申、酉、戌、亥,共十二个。十个天干与十二个地支一一组合,共形成了六十个基本单位,是古代用来纪年的重要方法。

Heavenly Stems and Earthly Branches

The heavenly stems and earthly branches were the basic units in ancient Chinese chronology. The 10 heavenly stems are *Jia*, *Yi*, *Bing*, *Ding*, *Wu*, *Ji*, *Geng*, *Xin*, *Ren* and *Gui*, while the 12 earthly branches are *Zi*, *Chou*, *Yin*, *Mao*, *Chen*, *Si*, *Wu*, *Wei*, *Shen*, *You*, *Xu* and *Hai*. Each of the 10 heavenly stems is paired up respectively with each of the 12 earthly branches, making a total of 60 basic units as the means to chronicle years in ancient times.

> 姓氏与寻根

《淮南子·原道训》中载："万物有所生，而独知守其根"。中华民族是世界上"寻根意识"最为强烈的族群。中国人无论走到哪里，都始终不忘寻找自己的"根"，不忘自己的祖宗和故乡。

随着个人或家族的迁移，姓氏人口的分布从发源地逐渐扩散到各地，甚至全世界，但人们始终不忘寻找宗脉源流和祖先的故乡，寻求血脉亲情和归属感。寻根问祖是中华民族的传统，作为一种礼仪传承至今。

故乡不仅仅是一个人出生的地方，更是其祖先诞生的地方、其姓氏起源的地方。因此，寻根问祖的过程也是寻找、探索、继承和发展家族文化的过程。中华民族是讲究

> Surnames and Root-searching

It is recorded in *Huai Nan Zi: Original Dao* (a miscellany of writing from the Western Han Dynasty, 206 B.C.-25 A.D.) that, "All beings are begotten while each knows to hold on to the root." Chinese people are the most root-minded nation in the world. Wherever Chinese people go, they will never forget to search for their root and will never forget their own ancestors and hometowns.

Due to migration of individuals or families, population distribution has spread surnames all over the world. However, Chinese people do not forget their patriarchal clan origins and their ancestor's hometown; people long for the sense of belonging in kinship and consanguinity. Searching for ancestral roots is a traditional of Chinese people. It has been passed on to modern times as a kind of ritual and etiquette.

团结的民族，同一姓氏作为一种血缘关系的标志，使人与人聚合在一起，使家族延续下去。在古代，很多家族十分重视健全本家族的文化，通过家谱、家祭、家训、家法、祠堂等方式，家族文化得以代代传承。

家谱又称"族谱""家乘""宗谱"，是一种以表谱的形

The hometown is not only a place where a person was born, but also the place where the ancestor and the surname originated. In this sense, the process of root-searching is also a process to search, probe, inherit and develop the clan culture. The Chinese nation is a nation with particular emphasis on solidarity. The shared surname, as a symbol of a blood relationship, will draw

- 黄帝拜祖大典（图片提供：FOTOE）
此为黄帝的故里——河南新郑举行的拜祖大典。黄帝故里祠始建于汉代，是海内外中国人寻根的圣地。

Huangdi Worship Ceremony
The ceremony is held at Huangdi's birth place at Xinzheng, Henan Province. First established in the Han Dynasty, the ancestral hall of Huangdi is the sacred land for all the Chinese to search for their roots.

宗祠祭祖（清）（图片提供：FOTOE）
Ancestral Hall Worshipping Ritual (Qing Dynasty, 1616-1911)

式记载以同一血缘关系为主体的家族世系繁衍和重要人物事迹的特殊资料。家谱与国史、地志并称为"中华民族的三大文献"。家谱不仅代表一种特殊的家族文化，更是寻根问祖、考定姓氏源流的重要参考资料。家谱源于历史上记载古代帝王、诸侯世系、事迹的谱学著作，早在魏晋南北朝时期就已产生，隋唐时期开始逐渐从官方流传到民间。

people together and sustain the lineage of the family and clan. In ancient times, many clans paid a lot of attention to systematizing the culture of their families and clans by means of family trees, family sacrificial rituals, family precepts, family codes and ancestral halls so that the family and clan culture could be carried on from generation to generation.

Family tree, also known as family pedigree or ancestral spectrum, is a special book in the form of a table to

家谱记载的家族以父系家族世系、人物为中心，一般分为世系图、正文、附录三个部分。世系图记录着本族中每个人的名字，是用于查证谱中某人的世系所承、属于什么时代、父亲是何人的图表，有北宋文学家欧阳修创立的欧式、北宋文学家苏洵创立的苏式、宝塔式和牒记式四种基本记述格式。正文

- 木雕龙纹家谱（图片提供：微图）
Wood Carving Family Tree with Dragon Pattern

record the genealogy of a family clan on the basis of blood relationships as well as the deeds of the important personages in the family or clan. Family tree, national history, and chorography are called the three major literatures of China. The family tree is not merely a special element of family culture, but also an important reference for root-searching and genealogical research. Family tree originated from the genealogical literature in antiquity, which kept track of the lineage and deeds of ancient emperors, kings and seigniors. They had already existed in as early as the Wei, Jin, Southern and Northern dynasties. It was during the Sui and Tang dynasties that family tree gradually spread from the official world to the civilian world.

The records in family trees are focused on the lineage of patriarchal figures and clans. There are generally three parts in a family tree: the genealogical chart, the main text and attachments. The genealogical chart, which records the name of each member of the clan, can be used to trace a person's genealogical line in the family tree including information about the time when the person was born and who his father was. There are four basic formats

是按世系图中所列人物的先后次序编定的，一般概括性地介绍人物的字号、父讳、行次、时代、职官、封爵、享年、卒日、谥号、姻配等。附录则记述了家族的迁徙、家族文化、族规、家训、郡望、堂号（家族的称号）等内容。

祭祖就是在祖先的诞生地、宗族祠堂或每个家庭内举行的祭祀祖先的礼仪。祭祖是中国人的一项传统的民俗活动，唐代时即有专人制定这种礼仪。祭祖一般在春节、清明节、中元节（农历七月十五）、中秋节（农历八月十五）、重阳节（农历九月初九）等传统节日进行。古人认为，祖先去世之后，其灵魂仍然存在，故将祖先视作"神灵"一样崇拜。因此在举行祭祖活动时，人们在表达对祖先的尊敬和怀念的同时，还祈求祖先保佑子孙平安。祭祖的仪式虽具有地域性差别，但大都包括在祖宗遗像前摆放水果、糕点等供品，点燃香烛，叩拜等。大型的祭祖活动还会有舞龙、舞狮、唢呐吹奏等文艺表演。

家训指治家、教子的名言警句，一般以家族和睦、孝顺父母、

for the illustrative records: the Ou-style genealogical chart, developed by Ouyang Xiu (1007-1072), a literary writer of the Northern Song Dynasty (960-1127); the Su-style chart, created by Su Xun (1009-1066), also a literary writer of the Northern Song Dynasty; the pagoda-style, and the tab-recorded style. The main text briefly describes each of the family members in the chart in order of precedence; their names and title names, deceased father's names, sibling order, official position, conferred feudal titles, life span, date of death, posthumous titles, spouses, and so on. The attachments keep records of the migration of the family and clan, clan culture, clan codes, family precepts, prefecture title, hall names (title of the clan), and other contents.

Ancestor worshipping rituals are ceremonies held at the birthplace of ancestors, the ancestral hall, or the family house. Ancestor worshipping is a folk custom in Chinese tradition dating back to the Tang Dynasty (618-907). It is usually held on such traditional festivals as the Spring Festival, Pure Brightness Festival (or Tomb-sweeping Festival), Hungry Ghost Festival (the 15th of the 7th month in Chinese lunar calendar), Mid-autumn Festival (15th of the 8th month

● 家庭祭祖（图片提供：FOTOE）
Family Ancestor Worshipping Ritual

尊敬长辈、礼义廉耻等内容为主。清初朱柏庐所撰的《朱子家训》（又名《朱子治家格言》）仅524字，从道德观念上劝人勤俭治家。

家法与家训不同，是家族成员必须服从的一种行为规范和规章制度，这与社会上的法律是同源的。旧时，如违反家族制定的家法，轻者被逐出家族，重者甚至被家族

in Chinese lunar calendar), and Double-ninth Festival (the 9th of the 9th month in Chinese lunar calendar). People in ancient times worshipped their ancestors like gods because they believed that the spirits of their ancestors still existed after they died. Therefore, ancestor-worshipping activities expressed not only people's respect for and memory of their ancestors, but also involved prayers for blessings for offspring. Although there are some regional differences in the ritual of ancestor-worshipping, it usually includes such activities as placing offerings of fruit, pastry, and the like in front of the portraits of ancestors, burning incense, kowtows, and so forth. A bigger worshipping event may include dragon dancing, lion dancing, *Suona* (a folk woodwind instrument) performances and other artistic shows.

Family precepts refer to sayings and aphorisms concerning how to manage a household and teach children. Usually, their contents may focus on family harmony, filial piety to parents, respect for seniors, sense of propriety, righteousness, honesty and honor, and the like. For example, the 524-word *Zhu's Family Instructions*, also known as *Zhuzi's Aphorism of Parental*

四川千佛寺千佛碑林石刻《朱子家训》
（图片提供：FOTOE）

Inscription of *Zhu's Family Instructions* at the Forest of Steles of Thousand-Buddha in Thousand-Buddha Temple, Sichuan Province

处死。

祠堂又称"家庙""宗祠"，是存放祖先牌位、举行家族内各种仪式和处理家族事务的地方。周代时，宗庙就已经出现，是帝王祭祀祖先的家庙，为帝王所专有。宋代时，理学家朱熹著《家礼》，提倡在民间建立家族宗祠供奉祖先，改称家庙为"祠堂"，对建筑布局也有明确的规制。明代以后，嘉靖皇帝"许民间皆得联宗立庙"，祠堂逐渐在各地流行起

Instructions, by Zhu Bolu from the early Qing Dynasty, is a famous family education book with a focus on family ethics.

Family codes are different from family precepts. They are a system of behavioral rules and regulations that members of a family or clan should abide by. They come from the same origin with social laws. In olden times, offenders of the family codes demanded by the clan might be expelled in the case of minor offenses, or even put to death in the case of serious violations.

The ancestral shrine, also called family temple or clan temple, is the place where the memorial tablets of deceased ancestors are kept, various rituals of the clan or family are held, and where clan affairs are handled. Since the Zhou Dynasty, ancestral shrines existed for the emperor's exclusive use to worship ancestors. In the Song Dynasty, Zhu Xi, a rationalist Neo-Confucian, greatly promoted in his book *Family*

来。清代时，山东、安徽、福建、广东等地出现了一些建筑精美、规模宏大的民间祠堂。

祠堂又可分为宗祠、支祠和家祠。宗祠为一宗合族的总祠，规模一般比较大，所祭祀的对象皆为始祖；分支、分房的为支祠；各个家庭供奉直系祖先的为家祠，又称"家堂"。各家族对本家族姓氏的源流和先祖的荣耀都极为重视，故而除了将之记录在族谱上，还会

Rituals the establishment of civilian ancestral shrines to worship ancestors. Family temples were therefore called ancestral shrines, with a clearly defined structure and layout. After the Ming Dynasty, when Emperor Jiajing allowed civilians to build clan temples for shared ancestral lineages, ancestral halls became popularized everywhere. In the Qing Dynasty (1616-1911), several grand structures of civilian ancestral shrines with exquisite architecture made their

- 安徽龙川村胡氏宗祠
  Hu's Clan Ancestral Shrine at Longchuan Village, Anhui Province

在家族祠堂的匾额上铭刻"尚书第""大夫第""进士第"等字样，彰显祖宗的显贵。

appearances in Shandong, Anhui, Fujian, Guangdong and other areas.

Ancestral shrines can be classified into the clan ancestral shrine, the branch ancestral shrine, and the family ancestral hall. The clan ancestral shrine is the headquarter temple of all the tribes of a clan. It is usually built with greater scale in dedication to the primogenitors of the clan. The branch ancestral shrines are those built by each branch clan. Family ancestral halls or family shrines are for families to worship immediate forebears. Each family and clan places much emphasis on the origin of their clans and surnames as well as the glory of their ancestors. Therefore, some ancestral shrines may have such titles as High Minister's House, Senior Minister's House, Imperial Scholar's House and others on the plaques to honor the dignity of their ancestors.

- "修德延贤"家训
  此门楼上所刻的"修德延贤"是近代浙江商人胡雪岩家的家训。
  Family Precept of Virtues Cultured to Perpetuate Sageness
  This inscription of Virtues Cultured to Perpetuate Sageness on the gate tower was the family precept of Hu Xueyan, a distinguished modern-time merchant of Zhejiang Province.

● 安徽西递胡氏支祠追慕堂
Memorial Hall of Hu's Branch Ancestral Shrine at Xidi Village, Anhui Province

祠堂的布局

祠堂的建筑布局可分为三种形式：一是以朱熹《家礼》为蓝本的祠堂，即在正寝之东设置四个龛位（供奉佛像、灵位等的小阁子），以奉高、曾、祖、考四世先祖，唐宋三品官家庙、宋元及明初的大部分祠堂均属此类。二是由先祖故居演变而来的祠堂，主要为祭祀分迁始祖及各门别祖的祠堂，其平面布局依各地民居模式的不同而不同。三是独立于居室的大型祠堂，其中轴线上的布置一般为大门—享堂—寝堂。享堂是祭祀祖先、举行仪式及族众聚会之所，寝堂则为安放祖先灵位之所。一些官宦世家或富商、巨贾往往还在祠堂前增建照壁、牌楼等物，十分精美。

- **北京太庙**

北京太庙是明、清两代皇帝祭祀祖先的宗庙，始建于1420年。

Imperial Ancestral Temple in Beijing

Built in 1420, the Imperial Ancestral Temple was the clan ancestral shrine for emperors of the Ming and Qing dynasties to worship ancestors.

Layout of Ancestral Shrines

The structural layout of the ancestral shrine can come in three different styles. The first one is modeled on the blueprint described in Zhu Xi's *Family Rituals* with four niches (small compartments for Buddha sculptures or spirit tablets) installed on the east side of the main chamber to worship the spirits of the four preceding generations, namely the deceased father, grandfather, great-grandfather and great-great-grand father. Family temples of rank-three officials from the Tang and Song dynasties as well as most of the ancestral shrines in the Song Dynasty, Yuan Dynasty and early Ming Dynasty belonged to this category. The second kind is ancestral shrines converted from the abodes of forebears. They are mainly ancestral shrines to worship extended forebears and ancestors. The floor plans are different according to local residence styles. The third kind is the large-scale ancestral shrines separate from the abode, the offering hall, and the chamber hall in line with the design axis. The offering hall is the place where spirits of ancestors are worshipped, rituals are held, and meetings are convened for the clan. The chamber hall is the place where the spirit tablets of ancestors are placed. Some families of hereditary officials or wealthy tycoons would build screen walls or archways in front of the ancestral shrines to add a spectacular touch.

洪洞大槐树

"问我祖先在何处？山西洪洞大槐树。祖先故居叫什么？大槐树下老鹳窝。"这首民谣数百年来在中国北方地区世代相传，海内外众多中国人将洪洞视为"家"，看作"根"。洪洞大槐树又称"古大槐树""山西大槐树"，位于山西洪洞县城西北两公里处的贾村。

明代初年，由于连年战乱，以及疫病流行、河水泛滥，中原、江南地区人口锐减。山西晋南是当时人口最为稠密的地区，而洪洞又是当时晋南最大、人口最多的县。《明史》《明实录》等史书记载，自洪武六年（1373年）到永乐十五年（1417年），这里先后进行过18次移民，即将山西境内的很多民众集中到洪洞，再分批迁往北京、河北、河南、山东、安徽、江苏、湖北、陕西、甘肃等地。

据记载，当时贾村西侧有一座广济寺，寺旁有一棵"树身数围，荫遮数亩"的

● 洪洞大槐树寻根祭祖处
（图片提供：FOTOE）
Root-searching and Ancestor-worshipping Place at Great Pagoda Tree of Hongtong

汉槐，汾河滩上的老鹳在树上构窝、筑巢。明政府在广济寺设局驻员，集中办理与移民相关的事宜，大槐树下就成了移民集聚之地。全国各地的很多地方志等都明确记载了在山西洪洞大槐树下办理的集中移民。

目前洪洞大槐树的祭祖堂里供奉着所有从大槐树下迁出去的姓氏的牌位，共有1230个。

Great Pagoda Tree of Hongtong

"If you ask me where my ancestors were, the answer lies in the Big Pagoda Tree of Hongtong in Shanxi. What is it called, the abode of the ancestors? The old stork nest below the Big Pagoda Tree." This folk ballad has been sung generation after generation in northern China for centuries. A lot of Chinese people consider this place as their home and root. The Great Pagoda Tree of Hongtong, also known as Ancient Great Pagoda Tree or Shanxi Great Pagoda Tree, is located at Jia Village two kilometers to the northwest of Hongtong County in Shanxi Province.

At the beginning of the Ming Dynasty, the population in the south of Yangtze River greatly dwindled because of long wars, epidemics, and flooding. The south of Shanxi Province had the greatest population density during that time, while Hongtong was the biggest and most populated prefecture in the south of Shanxi. According to descriptions in such historic books as *History of the Ming*, *The Memoir of the Ming Dynasty*, and the like, during the half century from the 6th year of Hongwu Period (1373) to the 15th year of Yongle Period (1417), a total of 18 waves of migration occurred. In other words, a large number of migrants in Shanxi Province gathered at Hongtong and then migrated in different batches to Hebei, Henan, Shandong, Anhui, Jiangsu, Hubei, Shaanxi and Gansu, etc.

According to records, there was a Guangji Temple at that time in the west of Jia Village. By the temple was a pagoda tree whose trunk size was so big that its shade covered several *Mu* (Chinese unit to measure land area). All the old storks on the bank of Fen River nestled in this tree. The government of the Ming Dynasty set up bureaus at Guangji Temple to handle matters of migration, so the big pagoda tree became the place where migrants gathered. Many chorographical literatures and local chronicles clearly record about the concentration of migrants under the Great Pagoda Tree of Hongtong in Shanxi.

Currently, the ancestral hall at the Great Pagoda Tree at Hongtong still accommodates the surname memorial tablets of those migrants. A total of 1,230 tablets bear the traces of those who migrated from Hongtong to all over the country.

细数中国姓氏
Introducing Chinese Surnames

　　姓氏是代表家族系统的符号，通过这个符号，每个人都可以把自己与历史、文化联系起来。每一个姓氏都源远流长、丰富多彩。

The surname is a consanguinity symbol of family systems. Through this symbol, people can link up oneself with history and culture. Every surname has a rich and colorful history that goes back to the distant past.

> 《百家姓》

提起中国姓氏，必然离不开中国人耳熟能详的《百家姓》。《百家姓》《三字经》《千字文》《幼学琼林》等都是中国古代孩童的启蒙读物。《百家姓》成书于北宋初年，作者不详，一般认为是吴越国（907—978）钱塘（今浙江杭州）的一位普通人所撰。吴越国是五代时期十个偏安一隅的小国中的一个，由临安（今浙江杭州）人钱镠创建。"赵钱孙李"成为《百家姓》前四姓，据说是因为当时宋朝的皇帝是赵氏、吴越国的国王是钱氏、吴越国王的正妃是孙氏、南唐（937—975）国王是李氏，故这四个姓氏被列在《百家姓》的前面。

《百家姓》中的"百"并不是确切的"一百个"的意思，而是个

> Book of Hundred Family Names

When speaking of Chinese surnames, one is bound to talk about the *Book of Hundred Family Names*, which Chinese people are very familiar with. The *Book of Hundred Family Names, Three-Character Classic, Thousand-Character Classic, Young School Collection,* and the like are all ancient Chinese education reading materials for children. The *Book of Hundred Family Names* was first published in the early years of the Northern Song Dynasty. Its anonymous author is generally considered to be a commoner from the State of Wuyue (907-978) in Qiantang (now Hangzhou of Zhejiang Province). First established by Qian Liu in Lin'an (now Hangzhou of Zhejiang Province), the State of Wuyue was one of the ten small countries that were content with their minor existence during the Five dynasties (907-960).

概数。现在的《百家姓》全书共有568个字，记载了504个姓氏，其中单姓为444个，复姓为60个。《百家姓》采用四言体例，句句押韵，排列次序不以人口数量的多少为依据，而是按照读来顺口、易学、好记来排列的。目前发现的最早的

According to a theory, the reason why Zhao, Qian, Sun and Li became the first four surnames in the *Book of Hundred Family Names* was that Zhao was the surname of the emperor of the Song Dynasty at the time, Qian was the surname of the king of Wuyue State, Sun was that of the imperial concubine to the

• 草书《百家姓》（清·成亲王）
Surnames Written in Cursive by Prince Cheng (Qing Dynasty, 1616-1911)

印刷体《百家姓》是在14世纪初，也就是元代出版的，根据汉字和蒙古字的语音、笔画对应排版而成。《百家姓》有多个版本，所收姓氏内容及数量都有差别。以下为当代一种常见的版本。

甲骨文姓氏对照表
A Contrast of Surnames between Oracle Bone Inscriptions and Modern Chinese Characters

king of Wuyue State, and Li was the king of the Southern Tang Dynasty (937-975). Therefore, these four surnames were listed at the beginning of the *Book of Hundred Family Names*.

The family names in the *Book of Hundred Family Names* do not literally mean that the book contains a hundred surnames. The current version contains a total of 568 words, of which 504 surnames are recorded, including 444 single-character surnames and 60 two-character surnames. The *Book of Hundred Family Names* is styled in four-word lines in rhyme, its sorting order not based upon the population size of the surnames but on the verbal fluency for the sake of easiness to read and memorize. The earliest printed copy of the *Book of Hundred Family Names* discovered so far was published in the early 14th century (Yuan Dynasty, 1206-1368), laid out in correspondence with the pronunciation and strokes of the Chinese and Mongolian characters. There are multiple versions of the *Book of Hundred Family Names*, and the content and number of collected surnames are different. The following is a common contemporary version.

● 甲骨文姓氏对照表 (图片提供：FOTOE)
Oracle Surname Comparison Table

《百家姓》正文
Text of the Book of Hundred Family Names

赵 钱 孙 李	周 吴 郑 王	冯 陈 褚 卫	蒋 沈 韩 杨
Zhao Qian Sun Li	Zhou Wu Zheng Wang	Feng Chen Chu Wei	Jiang Shen Han Yang
朱 秦 尤 许	何 吕 施 张	孔 曹 严 华	金 魏 陶 姜
Zhu Qin You Xu	He Lü Shi Zhang	Kong Cao Yan Hua	Jin Wei Tao Jiang
戚 谢 邹 喻	柏 水 窦 章	云 苏 潘 葛	奚 范 彭 郎
Qi Xie Zou Yu	Bo Shui Dou Zhang	Yun Su Pan Ge	Xi Fan Peng Lang
鲁 韦 昌 马	苗 凤 花 方	俞 任 袁 柳	酆 鲍 史 唐
Lu Wei Chang Ma	Miao Feng Hua Fang	Yu Ren Yuan Liu	Feng Bao Shi Tang
费 廉 岑 薛	雷 贺 倪 汤	滕 殷 罗 毕	郝 邬 安 常
Fei Lian Cen Xue	Lei He Ni Tang	Teng Yin Luo Bi	Hao Wu An Chang
乐 于 时 傅	皮 卞 齐 康	伍 余 元 卜	顾 孟 平 黄
Le Yu Shi Fu	Pi Bian Qi Kang	Wu Yu Yuan Bu	Gu Meng Ping Huang
和 穆 萧 尹	姚 邵 湛 汪	祁 毛 禹 狄	米 贝 明 臧
He Mu Xiao Yin	Yao Shao Zhan Wang	Qi Mao Yu Di	Mi Bei Ming Zang
计 伏 成 戴	谈 宋 茅 庞	熊 纪 舒 屈	项 祝 董 梁
Ji Fu Cheng Dai	Tan Song Mao Pang	Xiong Ji Shu Qu	Xiang Zhu Dong Liang
杜 阮 蓝 闵	席 季 麻 强	贾 路 娄 危	江 童 颜 郭
Du Ruan Lan Min	Xi Ji Ma Qiang	Jia Lu Lou Wei	Jiang Tong Yan Guo
梅 盛 林 刁	钟 徐 邱 骆	高 夏 蔡 田	樊 胡 凌 霍
Mei Sheng Lin Diao	Zhong Xu Qiu Luo	Gao Xia Cai Tian	Fan Hu Ling Huo
虞 万 支 柯	昝 管 卢 莫	经 房 裘 缪	干 解 应 宗
Yu Wan Zhi Ke	Zan Guan Lu Mo	Jing Fang Qiu Miao	Gan Xie Ying Zong
丁 宣 贲 邓	郁 单 杭 洪	包 诸 左 石	崔 吉 钮 龚
Ding Xuan Ben Deng	Yu Shan Hang Hong	Bao Zhu Zuo Shi	Cui Ji Niu Gong
程 嵇 邢 滑	裴 陆 荣 翁	荀 羊 於 惠	甄 麴 家 封
Cheng Ji Xing Hua	Pei Lu Rong Weng	Xun Yang Yu Hui	Zhen Qu Jia Feng
芮 羿 储 靳	汲 邴 糜 松	井 段 富 巫	乌 焦 巴 弓
Rui Yi Chu Jin	Ji Bing Mi Song	Jing Duan Fu Wu	Wu Jiao Ba Gong

043

细数中国姓氏

Introducing Chinese Surnames

《百家姓》正文
Text of the *Book of Hundred Family Names*

牧 隗 山 谷 Mu Wei Shan Gu	车 侯 宓 蓬 Che Hou Mi Peng	全 郗 班 仰 Quan Xi Ban Yang	秋 仲 伊 宫 Qiu Zhong Yi Gong
宁 仇 栾 暴 Ning Qiu Luan Bao	甘 钭 厉 戎 Gan Dou Li Rong	祖 武 符 刘 Zu Wu Fu Liu	景 詹 束 龙 Jing Zhan Shu Long
叶 幸 司 韶 Ye Xing Si Shao	郜 黎 蓟 薄 Gao Li Ji Bo	印 宿 白 怀 Yin Su Bai Huai	蒲 邰 从 鄂 Pu Tai Cong E
索 咸 籍 赖 Suo Xian Ji Lai	卓 蔺 屠 蒙 Zhuo Lin Tu Meng	池 乔 阴 郁 Chi Qiao Yin Yu	胥 能 苍 双 Xu Nai Cang Shuang
闻 莘 党 翟 Wen Shen Dang Zhai	谭 贡 劳 逄 Tan Gong Lao Pang	姬 申 扶 堵 Ji Shen Fu Du	冉 宰 郦 雍 Ran Zai Li Yong
郤 璩 桑 桂 Xi Qu Sang Gui	濮 牛 寿 通 Pu Niu Shou Tong	边 扈 燕 冀 Bian Hu Yan Ji	郏 浦 尚 农 Jia Pu Shang Nong
温 别 庄 晏 Wen Bie Zhuang Yan	柴 瞿 阎 充 Chai Qu Yan Chong	慕 连 茹 习 Mu Lian Ru Xi	宦 艾 鱼 容 Huan Ai Yu Rong
向 古 易 慎 Xiang Gu Yi Shen	戈 廖 庾 终 Ge Liao Yu Zhong	暨 居 衡 步 Ji Ju Heng Bu	都 耿 满 弘 Du Geng Man Hong
匡 国 文 寇 Kuang Guo Wen Kou	广 禄 阙 东 Guang Lu Que Dong	欧 殳 沃 利 Ou Shu Wuo Li	蔚 越 夔 隆 Wei Yue Kui Long
师 巩 厍 聂 Shi Gong She Nie	晁 勾 敖 融 Chao Gou Ao Rong	冷 訾 辛 阚 Leng Zi Xin Kan	那 简 饶 空 Na Jian Rao Kong
曾 毋 沙 乜 Zeng Wu Sha Nie	养 鞠 须 丰 Yang Ju Xu Feng	巢 关 蒯 相 Chao Guan Kuai Xiang	查 后 荆 红 Zha Hou Jing Hong
游 竺 权 逯 You Zhu Quan Lu	盖 益 桓 公 Gai Yi Huan Gong	万俟 司马 Moqi Sima	上官 欧阳 Shangguan Ouyang
夏侯 诸葛 Xiahou Zhuge	闻人 东方 Wenren Dongfang	赫连 皇甫 Helian Huangfu	尉迟 公羊 Yuchi Gongyang
澹台 公冶 Tantai Gongye	宗政 濮阳 Zongzheng Puyang	淳于 单于 Chunyu Chanyu	太叔 申屠 Taishu Shentu

《百家姓》正文
Text of the Book of Hundred Family Names

公孙 仲孙 Gongsun Zhongsun	轩辕 令狐 Xuanyuan Linghu	钟离 宇文 Zhongli Yuwen	长孙 慕容 Zhangsun Murong
鲜于 闾丘 Xianyu Lüqiu	司徒 司空 Situ Sikong	亓官 司寇 Qiguan Sikou	仉 督 子车 Zhang Du Ziju
颛孙 端木 Zhuansun Duanmu	巫马 公西 Wuma Gongxi	漆雕 乐正 Qidiao Yuezheng	壤驷 公良 Rangsi Gongliang
拓拔 夹谷 Tuoba Jiagu	宰父 谷梁 Zaifu Guliang	晋 楚 闫 法 Jin Chu Yan Fa	汝 鄢 涂 钦 Ru Yan Tu Qin
段干 百里 Duangan Baili	东郭 南门 Dongguo Nanmen	呼延 归 海 Huyan Gui Hai	羊舌 微生 Yangshe Weisheng
岳 帅 缑 亢 Yue Shuai Gou Kang	况 后 有 琴 Kuang Hou You Qin	梁丘 左丘 Liangqiu Zuoqiu	东门 西门 Dongmen Ximen
商 牟 佘 佴 Shang Mou She Nai	伯 赏 南宫 Bo Shang Nangong	墨 哈 谯 笪 Mo Ha Qiao Da	年 爱 阳 佟 Nian Ai Yang Tong
第五 言 福 Diwu Yan Fu	百 家 姓 终 End of the Book		

《三字经》《千字文》《幼学琼林》

　　《三字经》《千字文》和《幼学琼林》都是古代儿童的读物，以其通俗易懂、朗朗上口而成为千古流传的佳作。

　　《三字经》最早成书于南宋时期，相传为南宋学者王应麟（1223—1296）所著。《三字经》全书共一千一百四十五字，因以三字为一句，故名。《三字经》的内容十分广泛，包括历史、天文、地理、道德、民间传说等，古人有"熟读三字经，便可知天下事，通圣人礼"的说法。明代时，《三字经》出现了多种增补版本。

　　《千字文》成书于南朝梁武帝时期（502—549），梁武帝命人拓下王羲之所撰碑文上的一千个不重复的字，用于教育子侄。然而这一千个字杂乱无章，没有关联，很难记忆。于是梁武帝就让博学多才的周兴嗣编撰成文。周兴嗣将这一千个字（其中有一个"洁"字重复，实为九百九十九个字）编撰成为四字一句、富有韵律、通俗易懂的文章。《千字文》囊括了天文、地理、历史、饮食、起居、修身、养性、礼教等多方面的内容。后世对《千字文》有多种续编和改编。

《幼学琼林》为明代学者程登吉所著，又名《成语考》《故事寻源》。此书的内容涉及成语、典故、历史人物、天文、地理、典章、制度、风俗、礼仪、饮食、器用、宫室珍宝、鸟兽、花木等多个方面。古人有"读了《幼学》走天下"的说法。

Three-Character Classic, Thousand-Character Classic, Young School Collection

The *Three-Character Classic*, *Thousand-Character Classic*, and *Young School Collection* were the reading primers for children's education in the old times. Since they are popular, comprehensible, and easy to recite, they have become masterpieces through time.

The *Three-Character Classic* was published in the Southern Song Dynasty (1127-1279). The anonymous author is generally believed to be Wang Yinglin (1223-1296) from the Southern Song Dynasty. The *Three-Character Classic*, which contains more than 1,145 words, was named because of the use of three characters in each line. The extensive contents of the *Three-Character Classic* cover history, astronomy, geography, ethics, folklore, and so forth. It was a widespread idea among people of ancient times that "those versed in the *Three-Character Classic* understand everything in the world and know all the etiquette of sage". During the Ming Dynasty (1368-1644), a variety of supplemented versions of *Three-Character Classic* appeared.

The *Thousand-Character Classic* was composed in the Southern dynasties when Emperor Wu of Liang ordered people (502-549) to make rubbings of a thousand different characters from Wang Xizhi's inscriptions and used them to teach his sons and nephews. However, these thousand characters were disorganized, non-related and difficult to remember, so the erudite scholar Zhou Xingsi took up the job to re-organize the words (among them, the character of *Jie* was repeated several times, therefore making it a total of 999 different words in reality) into an article of four-character rhyming lines, making it popular and easy to understand. The *Thousand-Character Classic* encompasses a wide variety of contents, such as astronomy, geography, history, daily life and diet, self-cultivation, the Confucian code of ethics, and so on. Later generations had different supplemented versions of the *Thousand-Character Classic*.

Compiled in the Ming Dynasty, the *Young School Collection* by Cheng Dengji was also known as *Annotated Book of Idioms* or *Origins of Stories*. The collection covers a variety of contents, including proverbs and allusions, historical figures, astronomy and geography, laws and institutions, customs and rituals, diet and utensils, palace treasures, flora and fauna, and so forth. People once believed that "study of the *Young School Collection* would help one know the world".

> 常见姓氏

中国历史上曾出现过20000多个姓氏，现已普查到的有4000多个。目前，中国乃至全世界范围内华人使用较多的姓氏有10个，是中国姓氏中最为常见的代表姓氏。在中国，这些姓氏集中分布的地域不同，北方的常见姓氏有张、王、李、赵、刘，南方的常见姓氏有陈、黄、杨、周、吴。中国人数最多的十个姓是李、王、张、刘、陈、杨、赵、黄、周和吴。

李姓

目前，李姓人口在中国姓氏中排第一。

李姓发源于河南，随着人口的不断增加，李姓族人开始向各地迁移。西汉时期，李姓族人已迁移至

> Common Surnames

More than 20,000 surnames have appeared over the course of Chinese history, and current surveys estimate 4,000-plus surnames. Presently, there are ten surnames that are commonly used by Chinese people in China and around the world. These ten surnames are the most representative Chinese surnames. In China, these surnames are distributed differently in concentration so that Zhang, Wang, Li, Zhao and Liu are most commonly seen in the North, while Chen, Huang, Yang, Zhou and Wu are commonly seen in the South. The ten major surnames that are most used are Li, Wang, Zhang, Liu, Chen, Yang, Zhao, Huang, Zhou and Wu.

Li

The surname Li ranks the first among Chinese surnames in terms of population.

• **黄河** (图片提供：全景正片)
中国第二大河，与长江并称为中国的"母亲河"，是中华民族的主要发源地。发源于青藏高原的巴颜喀拉山脉北麓，呈"几"字形，自西向东注入渤海，全长5464千米。

The Yellow River
The second largest river in China, known as the Mother River of China along with the Yangtze River. It is the birthplace of Chinese people. Originating from the north of the Bayan Har Mountains of the Qinghai-Xizang Plateau, the Yellow River runs along in the shape of the Chinese character "几" (*Ji*), extending from the west to the east for a total of 5,464 km before joining the Bohai Sea.

● 长江（图片提供：全景正片）
中国第一大河、世界第三大河，发源于青藏高原，自西向东注入东海，全长6397千米。

The Yangtze River
The largest river in China and the third largest in the world. Originating from the Qinghai-Xizang Plateau, it runs a total length of 6,397 km from the west to the east and enters into the East China Sea.

山东、江西等地。在唐代，李姓为国姓，姓氏人口在全国范围内都有分布。北宋末年，北方的金兵入侵中原，受战争影响，北方的李姓族人纷纷向长江以南迁移。此次迁移是历史上迁移人数较多、规模较大的一次。在明代初年山西洪洞大槐树的人口大迁移中，李姓族人是主要的迁民，被分迁到河北、江苏、浙江、福建、广东、广西等地。如今，李姓人口遍布全中国，以河南、山东、四川等地居多。

- 甲骨文"李"

Character of *Li* in Oracle Bone Script

Originating in Henan, the surname of Li began to migrate to different places as its population increased. In the Western Han Dynasty, Li had migrated to Shandong, Jiangxi and other areas. During the Tang Dynasty when Li became the imperial surname, the population with the surname of Li was distributed nationwide. In the final years of the Northern Song Dynasty, when the army of Jin in the north invaded the Central Plains, the Li's clansmen in the north, driven by wars, moved one after another to the south of the Yangtze River. This migration was the largest in history with the most population relocated. At the beginning of the Ming Dynasty, the surname of Li composed the majority of the population during the Great Migration of the Great Pagoda Tree of Hongtong in Shanxi, where they moved and spread to Hebei, Jiangsu, Zhejiang, Fujian, Guangdong, Guangxi and other provinces. Nowadays, Li can be found all over China, with the most of them inhabiting in Henan, Shandong and Sichuan.

Origin of Li

There are two main origins for the surname of Li. The first one is derived from the surname of Ying, and the

姓氏起源

李姓的源头主要有两个：一是出自嬴姓，二是出自赐姓和改姓。

出自嬴姓。传说中，颛顼是黄帝的后代，为东夷族的部族首领。到了尧帝时期，颛顼氏族变成了八个分支，其中一支部落的首领名叫皋陶，官职大理（掌管刑狱的官）。皋陶的儿子伯益因辅佐大禹治理黄河水患有功，被赐嬴姓；其后代则世袭大理一职，同时以祖先的官职为姓，始为理姓。在商代末年，纣王昏庸无能，大臣理征因直言进谏被杀，他的儿子理利贞为了避免灾祸，只好逃亡。在逃亡的路上，理利贞靠吃李子来充饥。为了表达对李子的感激之情，他便改"理"姓为"李"姓。

出自赐姓和改姓。李渊是唐代的开国皇帝，他开创了长达近三百年的唐王朝。在此期间，帝王赐姓之风盛行，被赐姓的既有立下战功的汉族将领，也有少数民族部落首领。如唐肃宗时，将领董秦因有战功而被赐名为李忠臣。鲜卑族部落首领拓跋赤辞向唐王朝进贡，被赐姓李，改名为李赤辞。

other is either a conferred surname or a changed surname.

Originating from the surname of Ying: As the descendant of Huangdi in legend, Zhuanxu was the leader of the Dongyi Tribe. During the reign of Emperor Yao, the clan of Zhuanxu divided into eight branches, among which was a tribe with its leader named Gao Yao holding the official position of chief magistrate, Dali (an officer in charge of punishments and imprisonments). Due to his success in assisting Yu the Great to solve the flooding problems of the Yellow River, Bo Yi, Gao Yao's son, was bestowed with the surname of Ying, and his descendants were hereditarily entitled to the post of Dali. His descendants later began to use their ancestors' official title, Li, as their surname. In the final years of the Shang Dynasty, Minister Li Zheng was killed due to his blatant remonstrations against the fatuous and incompetent King Zhou of Shang. In order to avoid the coming persecution, his son, Li Lizhen, had to flee. During his flee, Li Lizhen had to rely on plums (*Lizi* in Chinese) to quench his hunger and thirst. In order to express his gratitude to the plums, he changed the character

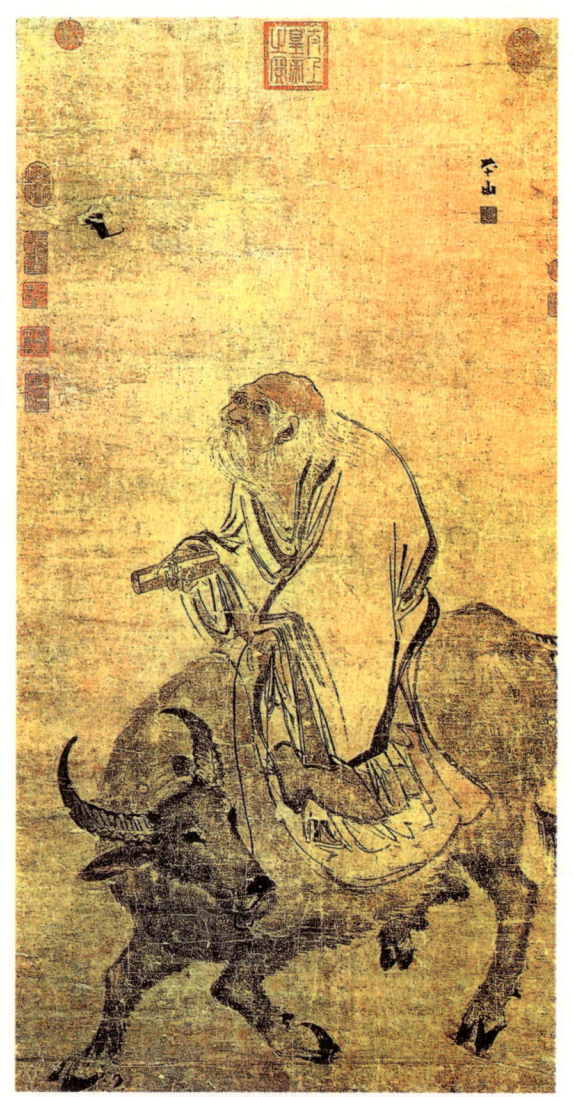

《老子骑牛图》（明·张路）

老子被道教奉为开山鼻祖，又称"道德天尊""太上老君"，大青牛是他的坐骑。

Portrait of Laozi Riding An Ox, by Zhang Lu (Ming Dynasty, 1368-1644)

Worshipped as the Taoist founder, Laozi was also known as the Holy Man of Virtues and Ultimate High Lord. The big green ox served as his mount.

of his surname to that of the fruit, both pronounced *Li*.

Conferred or changed surname: Li Yuan, the founding emperor of the Tang Dynasty, ushered in the nearly 300-year-long reign of the Tang Dynasty. During this period, the tradition of conferring the imperial surname prevailed. Those conferred with the imperial surname included not only Han generals who had accomplished military achievements but also leaders of tribes. For example, during the reign of Emperor Suzong of Tang, General Dong Qin was conferred with the name of Li Zhongchen due to his military achievements, and Tuoba Chici, leader of the Xianbei Tribe, was given the imperial surname when he was paying his tributes to the Tang Dynasty, his converted name being Li Chici.

Surnames of ethnic groups such as the Zhuang, Miao, Yao, Bai, Yi, Tujia and other ethnic groups were also gradually converted to Han surnames during the process of their integration with the Han culture. Some of them changed to Li.

Famous Personages Surnamed Li in History

Li Er was born in the State of Chu during the Spring and Autumn Period. In

壮族、苗族、瑶族、白族、彝族、土家族等少数民族在与汉族进行文化融合的过程中，也逐渐开始使用汉族姓氏，其中一些人便改姓李。

李姓历史名人

李耳，春秋时期楚国人。春秋时期，人们尊称学识渊博的人为"子"，李耳因博学多识，被称为"老子"。老子是中国古代伟大的思想家、哲学家和道家的创始人，著有《道德经》一书。老子在其著作《道德经》中提出了朴素的辩证法，主张无为而治，即顺应自然变化，不妄自作为而使天下得到治理。

李清照（1084—1155），号易安居士，南宋著名女词人。她出生在一个书香世家，婚后与丈夫赵明诚一起从事金石书画的搜集和整理工作。然而随着金兵入侵中原，战火不断，李清照的人生发生了转折，一家人颠沛流离。丈夫途中病死后，她的境遇更加困苦。因此，她的词作分为前期、后期两个阶段：前期多描写悠闲、舒适的爱情生活及自然景物，韵调优美，如《一剪梅·红藕香残玉簟秋》；后

the Spring and Autumn Period, people respectfully referred to knowledgeable people as Zi. As a learned individual, Li Er was also honored as Laozi. Laozi was a great thinker, philosopher and founder of Taoism in ancient China. He was also the writer of the book Daodejing: Classic of the Way and Virtue. In Daodejing: Classic of the Way and Virtue, Laozi proposed a simple dialectic and advocated governance by non-interference, an idea to conform to natural changes without assertive intervention so the world would eventually fall into orderly control.

As a well-known poetess in the Southern Song Dynasty, Li Qingzhao (1084-1155), with the title name of Yi'an. Raised in a scholarly family, she later married Zhao Mingcheng and worked together with her husband on collecting and organizing works of epigraphy, seal cutting and calligraphy. However, due to the invasion of the Jin army in the Central Plains and the continuous wars, a turning point occurred in Li Qingzhao's life when her family drifted from place to place and her husband died of illness en route, driving her into bitter hardship. As a result of this, her poetry could be divided into the early and late stages. Most of her poems from the early stage

期多以慨叹身世、怀乡忆旧为主，韵调悲伤，如《声声慢·寻寻觅觅》。代表作有《声声慢》《一剪梅》《如梦令》《醉花阴》《武陵春》《夏日绝句》等。

described a relaxed and comfortable life of love coupled with natural scenery, such as *A Cutoff Twig of Plum: Red Lotus and Incense Residue with a Jade Bamboo Mat in an Autumn Day*. Most of her later poems contained themes of lamentation about life experiences, homesickness, and nostalgia for the past, such as *Slow in Sound: Search and Search*. Her signature poems include *Slow in Sound*, *A Cutoff Twig of Plum*, *Song like a Dream*, *Drunk Under the Shade of Flowers*, *Spring in Wuling* and *Summer Quatrains*.

- 李清照像
  Portrait of Li Qingzhao

奚墨变李墨

　　南北朝时，河北易水出产的墨质量上乘，被当时的书画家称为"易水墨"。唐中期爆发了安史之乱，河北易水的名墨工奚超带着全家逃到了安徽的歙州。歙州的山上长满了松树，而且这种松树的松油非常多，是制墨的上等材料。奚超决定在此地定居，重操旧业。他的大儿子廷珪在制墨时大胆创新，发明了胶不变质、墨不变形、光泽如漆的墨，时人称之为"廷珪墨"。后来，南唐后主李煜得到了廷珪墨，一用即视为珍宝。于是他下旨封廷珪墨为国墨，同时赐给奚家国姓"李"，并封廷珪为墨务官。从此，奚廷珪成为李廷珪，"奚墨"变成了"李墨"。

- 《十六罗汉图》墨（清）

墨又称"墨锭"，其主要原料有炭黑、松烟、胶等。墨是书画家写字、画画时用的颜料，加适当的水研磨成墨汁后即可使用。

Ink Stick: *Portrait of Sixteen Arhats* (Qing Dynasty, 1616-1911)

The ink, also known as the ink stick, was primarily made of such raw materials as carbon blacks, pine soot and gum. The ink was the main pigment used by painters and calligraphers in their writings and paintings. In its usage, an appropriate amount of water must be added so that the ink can be obtained by grinding in the water.

Xi's Ink Changed into Li's Ink

During the Southern and Northern dynasties, quality ink was produced in Yishui of Hebei Province. They were favored and called at that time by calligraphers and painters as Yishui's Ink. When the An Shi Rebellion (755-763) broke out in the middle of Tang Dynasty, a famous ink maker in Yishui named Xi Chao took his family and fled to Shezhou in Anhui Province. At the time, the mountains of Shezhou were covered with a special species of pine trees which yielded rich pine oil, the finest material for making ink. Xi Chao decided to settle down there and resume the production of ink. His eldest son, Tinggui, made bold innovations and produced a kind of ink with a lustrous appearance and that would not deform with its durable gum. People at the time called it Tinggui's Ink. Later, when Emperor Li Yu of the Southern Tang Dynasty came by the Tinggui's Ink and used it, he recognized it as a treasure. He then conferred Tinggui's Ink the title of National Ink and conferred the imperial surname Li on the Xi's family. Meanwhile, Tinggui was assigned the position as the ink officer. Thenceforth, Xi Tinggui became Li Tinggui, and Xi's Ink became Li's Ink.

王姓

目前，王姓人口在中国姓氏中排第二。

王姓最早活跃于山西、山东、河南等地。西晋末年战乱不断，王姓族人开始大举南迁，在湖北、江苏、浙江等地均有分布。在明代初年山西洪洞大槐树的人口大迁移中，王姓族人是主要的迁民，被分迁至河南、河北、山东、浙江、甘肃等地。如今，王姓人口主要分布在河南、四川、辽宁、黑龙江、山东、安徽、江苏、浙江等地。

Wang

At present, Wang ranks second among Chinese surnames in terms of population size.

The surname of Wang was first populated in Shanxi, Shandong, Henan and other regions. Due to the ongoing war at the end of the Western Jin Dynasty (265-317), the Wang clansmen began south-bound mass migrations and spread across regions including Hubei, Jiangsu and Zhejiang. During the early Ming Dynasty, the Wangs were also among the major migration clans in the Great Migration of the Great Pagoda Tree of

姓氏起源

王姓的源头主要有三个：一是出自子姓，二是出自姬姓，三是出自赐姓和改姓。

出自子姓。商代末年，纣王暴虐，昏庸无道，民不聊生。纣王的叔父，时任少师的比干冒死进谏，最终被纣王挖心处死。比干姓子，是商族祖先子契的后代，也是商朝皇族的王子。其子孙为了纪念他，遂以"王"为姓。

出自姬姓。东周时期，流经都城洛邑（今河南洛阳）的谷水、洛水两条河流经常泛滥。太子姬晋直

- 甲骨文"王"
  Character of *Wang* in Oracle Bone Script

Hongtong in Shanxi, and mostly relocated in Henan, Hebei, Shandong, Zhejiang, and Gansu provinces. Nowadays, the Wang population is located mainly in Henan, Sichuan Liaoning, Heilongjiang, Shandong, Anhui, Jiangsu and Zhejiang.

Origin of Wang

There are three main origins for the surname of Wang. The first is from the surname of Zi, the second is from the surname of Ji, and the third is either a conferred surname or a changed surname.

Originating from the surname of Zi: In the late Shang Dynasty when King Zhou ruled with tyranny and fatuity, the people had no means to live. Bigan, King Zhou's uncle and the prime minister, risked his own life by remonstrating and ended up being executed and had his heart ripped out by King Zhou. Bigan, surnamed Zi, the descendant of the Shang ancestor Zi Xie, was himself a prince (*Wangzi*) of the Shang Dynasty. In order to commemorate him, his children and grandchildren then took on the surname Wang (prince).

Originating from the surname of Ji: During the Eastern Zhou Dynasty (770 B.C.-256 B.C.), the two rivers, River Gu and River Luo, which flowed through Luoyi, the imperial city (now Luoyang,

言进谏，主张治水要因势利导，但被周灵王以忤逆罪废除太子之位，贬为庶民。姬晋举家从都城洛邑迁往山东琅邪（今山东临沂一带）。后来他的儿子在当地担任地方官司徒，因看到周王室日渐衰微，就辞去官职归隐山西太原。因他出生于王族，当地人便称他为"王家"，姬晋的后代遂以"王"为姓。

出自赐姓和改姓。丹是战国时期燕国的太子，姬姓。他因派荆轲刺杀秦始皇嬴政而被杀。到了西汉时期，外戚王莽篡夺汉王朝的政权建立了新朝（9—23），他便将自己的姓氏"王"赐予丹的玄孙嘉。同时，他还赐予对他篡夺汉政权有功的三十二名刘氏族人"王"姓。

除了汉族改姓，古代少数民族与汉族融合，受到汉族文化的影响，也常改姓汉族姓，其中便有改姓王的，例如汉代的匈奴人、唐代的契丹人等。

王姓历史名人

王羲之（303—361），字逸少，因担任右军将军，又称"王右军"，为东晋时期著名的书法

Henan Province), often caused flooding. Prince Ji Jin remonstrated and advocated to make the best of the circumstances to improve water management. He was instead stripped of his title by King Ling of Zhou in the name of disobedience, and thus became a commoner. Ji Jin relocated his entire family from the capital of Luoyi to Langya in Shandong (now Linyi of Shandong Province). Later, his son assumed a local position as the minister of personnel (*Situ*). Witnessing the decline of the imperial family of the Zhou Dynasty, he resigned from his post and led a hermit life in Taiyuan, Shanxi Province. Since he came from the king's family, many local people called them the Wang's (king) Family. Thence on, Ji Jin's offspring took on the surname of Wang.

Conferred or changed surname: Dan, surnamed Ji, was the prince of the State Yan during the Warring States Period (475 B.C.-221 B.C.). He was killed after his assassin, Jing Ke, failed the assassination targeting the king of the State Qin, Ying Zheng. By the time of the Western Han Dynasty when Wang Mang, a maternal relative of the emperor, usurped the throne and established the Xin Dynasty (9-23), he conferred his own surname on Dan's great-great-grandson,

家，有"书圣"的美誉。王羲之年少时师从书法家卫铄，后又学习书法家张芝的草书和书法家钟繇的正书（即小楷）。王羲之的成就主要是楷书、行书和草书，他独创了圆转、流利的书法风格。其主要作品有行书《兰亭集序》《快雪时晴帖》，草书《初月帖》，正书《黄庭经》《乐毅论》等。

• 王羲之像
Portrait of Wang Xizhi

Jia. At the same time, he also gave his surname Wang to 32 followers surnamed Liu for their assistance in usurping the throne of the Han Dynasty.

In addition to the Han people changing their surnames, in Chinese history, some ethnic groups interacted and communicated with the Han people and were influenced by Han culture, often changing their surnames to Han surnames. For example, some people from the Huns in the Han Dynasty and the Khitan Tribe in the Tang Dynasty changed their surnames to Wang.

Famous Personages Surnamed Wang in History

Wang Xizhi (303-361), with the courtesy name of Yishao, was also known as Wang Youjun for his position as the general of the right army. He was a celebrated calligrapher in the Eastern Jin Dynasty (317-420), and enjoyed the reputable title of Sage of Calligraphy. In his childhood, Wang Xizhi studied calligraphy under calligrapher Wei Shuo. Later, he learned the cursive script from calligrapher Zhang Zhi, and the regular script (i.e. regular script in small characters) from calligrapher Zhong Yao. Wang Xizhi's skills were mainly seen in regular, running and cursive scripts with

- **墨池石碑** (图片提供：FOTOE)

传说，王羲之经常在一个水池边练习书法，并用池水清洗砚台，长年累月，池水变成了黑色，故名"墨池"。此石碑上的"墨池"二字为宋代大书法家米芾所书。

Inscription of "墨池" (Ink Pond) on Stone Tablet

According to legends, Wang Xizhi frequently practiced calligraphy by a pond. After many years of cleaning his ink slab in the pond, the water in the pond became entirely black, hence the name Ink Pond. The words "墨池" on this stone tablet were wrote by the great calligrapher Mi Fu of the Song Dynasty (960-1279).

王昭君，名嫱，字昭君，是汉元帝时期的宫女。她虽进宫多年，却一直没有见过汉元帝，受尽冷落。当时，汉朝与北方民族匈奴之间常有战事发生，边疆不得安宁。公元前33年，匈奴首领呼韩邪单于主动请求和亲，对汉称臣。王昭

his unique rounded and fluent calligraphy style. His major works include *Preface to the Poems Composed at the Orchid Pavilion* and the calligraphy model *Clear Day After Brief Snow* written in running script, *In the First Month* in cursive script, as well as *Classic of Yellow Court* and *On Yue Yi* in regular script.

Wang Zhaojun, given name Qiang, title name Zhaojun, was a maid in the imperial court during the time of Emperor Yuan of the Han Dynasty. Despite being in the palace for many years, she never met Emperor Yuan of Han and was totally neglected. At the time, conflict between the Han Dynasty and the northern Huns Tribe occurred so frequently that the borders never saw peace. In 33 B.C., the Huns leader, Huhanye Chanyu, took

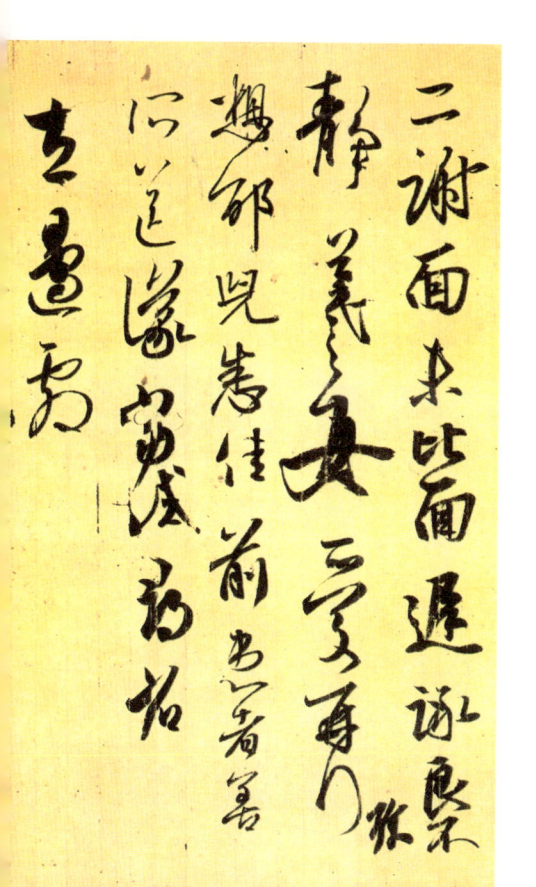

- 《二谢帖》（唐摹本）

东晋书法家王羲之未有书法真迹传世，《二谢帖》为唐代摹本。此帖书法为行草，共三十六个字。其书法风格为时草时行，体势间杂。

Calligraphy: *Two Xies* (Replica of the Tang Dynasty, 618-907)

There are no authentic works by the calligrapher Wang Xizhi of the Eastern Jin Dynasty (317-420) that has been handed down. The *Two Xies* is a copy from the Tang Dynasty. Written in running-cursive script, it contains a total of thirty-six characters in an intermingled style alternating between running and cursive scripts.

君接受了和亲的任务，随和亲队伍北上前往匈奴，史称"昭君出塞"。王昭君来到匈奴，受到当地人民的盛大欢迎，并被呼韩邪单于封为"宁胡阏氏"（阏氏即匈奴君主的妻子）。

the initiative to request a marriage for peace in submission to the Han Dynasty. Wang Zhaojun accepted the task of marriage, and was escorted by the Hun's peacemaking team to travel north to the tribe. It is known in history as Zhaojun's Departure from the Frontier. When she arrived at the territory of the Huns, Wang Zhaojun was greatly welcomed by the local people, and was later dubbed by Huhanye Chanyu as the Ninghu Yanzhi (Yanzhi means the wife of the king of Huns).

- 王昭君像

据说，在前往匈奴和亲的路上，萧瑟的景色和离别故土的悲伤使王昭君不由得弹奏起了悲伤的琵琶曲。天上南飞的大雁看到如此美丽、动人的女子，竟忘了扇动翅膀，掉了下来。

Portrait of Wang Zhaojun

According to legends, the bleak scenery on the route to the Huns and the sadness of parting with the homeland prompted Wang Zhaojun to play a sad tune with her *Pipa* (a 4-string Chinese lute). Upon seeing such a beautiful woman, the goose flying south forgot to flap its wings and fell from the sky.

荆轲刺秦王

荆轲刺秦王的记载最早见于《战国策》，讲述了战国末期刺客荆轲刺杀秦王嬴政的故事。

战国末年，秦国逐渐强大，实力远远超过韩、赵、燕、魏、楚、齐诸侯国。从公元前230年开始，秦国全面发动了兼并六国的统一战争。公元前227年，燕太子丹花重金找到刺客荆轲，让他携带樊於期的头颅和燕国督亢一带的地图，以投降的名义归顺秦国，以伺机刺杀秦王。荆轲临行前，燕太子丹和他的宾客都前往易水送别荆轲，荆轲唱出了"风萧萧兮易水寒，壮士一去兮不复还"的悲壮歌词，来表示自己刺杀秦王的决心。秦王嬴政在咸阳宫接见了荆轲。荆轲将匕首藏在了地图中，在给秦王奉上地图的时候，图穷匕首现，荆轲挥动匕首刺杀秦王，未中，反被左右的武士杀死。

荆轲
Jing Ke

匕首
Dagger

秦王
King of Qin, Ying Zheng

秦王武士
King's Guard

- 荆轲刺秦王画像石拓本（汉）（图片提供：FOTOE）
Stone Rubbing of the Portrait of *First Emperor of Qin and Jing Ke the Assassin* (Han Dynasty, 206 B.C.-220 A.D.)

First Emperor of Qin and Jing Ke the Assassin

The earliest tale of the First Emperor of Qin and Jing Ke the Assassin, was recorded in the history book *Strategies of the Warring States*. It relates the historical story of the attempted assassination of the First Emperor of Qin by Jing Ke, an assassin sent by the State of Yan during the late Warring States Period.

Toward the end of the Warring States Period, the State of Qin gradually grew far more powerful than the other vassal states of Han, Zhao, Yan, Wei, Chu and Qi. Starting from 230 B.C., Qin launched a comprehensive war of reunification against the six other states. In 227 B.C., Prince Dan of Yan spent a huge sum of money hiring the assassin Jing Ke to bring along with him the head of Fan Wuqi, and a map of the Yan State to visit Qin as a token of submission and surrender while harboring an attempt to assassinate the King of Qin. On Jing Ke's departure, Prince Dan of Yan and his guests bade farewell to Jing Ke as he chanted the tragic verse "rustling is the wind and cold is the water of Yi River; once gone, the heroic man will never return" to express his determination to kill the King of Qin. Ying Zheng, the King of Qin, greeted Jing Ke at the imperial palace in Xianyang, capital of Qin. Jing Ke hid a dagger in the map and assassinated Ying Zheng when the map was spread out and the dagger was exposed. Jing Ke failed to kill him. Instead, he was killed by nearby guards.

张姓

目前，张姓人口在中国姓氏中排第三。

秦汉时期，张姓族人从发源地古冀州（古时被称为"九州之首"，今河北衡水的一个县级市）分迁至各地。在明代初年山西洪洞大槐树的人口大迁移中，张姓族人是主要的迁民，被分迁至黑龙江、吉林、辽宁等地。如今，张姓人口

Zhang

At present, Zhang ranks the third among Chinese surnames in terms of population size.

During the Qin and Han dynasties, clans with the surname of Zhang moved from their birthplace at the ancient Jizhou County known as the Top of Nine Counties (*Zhou* is an ancient administrative division in ancient times, now a county-level city in Hengshui City

金文 "张"
Character of *Zhang* in Oracle Bone Script

主要分布在河北、河南、山东、四川、江苏、辽宁等地。

姓氏起源

张姓的源头主要有三个：一是出自姬姓，二是出自赐姓，三是由他姓而改。

出自姬姓。张姓有两个始祖，一是传说中黄帝的后代挥，二是春秋时期的晋国士大夫解张。《新唐书》记载："黄帝子少昊青阳氏第五子挥为弓正，始制弓矢，子孙赐姓张氏。"挥是黄帝儿子少昊的第五个儿子，担任弓正一职，是弓

of Hebei Province) to various places. In the early Ming Dynasty, the Zhangs were also among the major migration clans in the Great Migration of the Great Pagoda Tree of Hongtong in Shanxi, and were mostly relocated in Heilongjiang, Jilin and Liaoning. Today, the population with the surname of Zhang is distributed mainly in Hebei, Henan, Shandong, Sichuan, Jiangsu and Liaoning.

Origin of Zhang

There are three main origins for the surname Zhang. The first is from the surname of Ji, the second is a conferred surname, and the third is changed from other surnames.

Originating from the surname of Ji: There are two ancestors, one is Hui, a descendant of Huangdi in legend, and the other is Xie Zhang, a scholar-bureaucrat of the State of Jin in the Spring and Autumn Period. According to the records in *New Book of Tang*, "Hui, the fifth son of Shaohao, a descendant of the Huangdi, was the minister of bows, from whom the production of bows and arrows started. His offspring was therefore conferred with the surname of Zhang (In Chinese, Zhang is '张', and bow is '弓')." Hui is the fifth son of Huangdi's son Shaohao. As the inventor of bows and arrows, he

• 山西洪洞大槐树移民壁画（图片提供：瀛图）
Immigrant's Murals at the Great Pagoda of Hongtong in Shanxi

箭的发明者。后来其子孙被黄帝赐姓张。解张是春秋时期晋国的士大夫，他的祖先是周成王姬诵的儿子姬良。解张字张侯，其后代为了纪念他，便以其字为姓，始为张姓。

出自赐姓。三国时期，蜀汉丞相诸葛亮带领军队南征，降服了云南境内的酋长龙佑那，并赐他张姓，又称"张龙佑那"。唐代帝王曾赐予奚族张姓。奚族是中国北方

held the post of archery officer. Later, his children and grandchildren were conferred with the surname of Zhang by Huangdi. Xie Zhang was a scholar of the State of Jin in the Spring and Autumn Period. His ancestor, Ji Liang, was the son of King Cheng of Zhou, Ji Song. Since Xie Zhang's courtesy name was Zhang Hou, his descendants used his courtesy name as their family surname to commemorate him.

的古老民族，源于商周时期，于金代时灭亡。

由他姓而改。三国时期，魏国名将张辽原姓聂，为避灾祸改姓张，其后代遂以"张"为姓。

此外，还有一些经过汉化的少数民族也改姓汉族姓，阿昌族、纳西族、傈僳族、瑶族、壮族、黎族、高山族、藏族等少数民族中的一些人便以"张"为姓。

张姓历史名人

张仲景，东汉末年的著名医学家。他广泛收集药方，并确立了"六经辨证"的治疗原则，撰写出了传世医学巨著《伤寒杂病论》，被誉为"医圣"。他确立的"六经辨证"原则开辨证论治之先河，形成了独特的中国医学思想体系，成为中医临床上的基本原则。《伤寒杂病论》除了熔理、法、方、药于一炉，还阐述了作者"上以疗君亲之疾，下以救贫贱之厄，中以保身长全，以养其生"的济世思想，受历代医家推崇。

张三丰，道教的重要代表人物，名全一，一名君宝，又号玄玄子。其名字中的"三"代表阳，在

Originating from the conferred surname: Prime Minister Zhuge Liang of the State of Shu in the Three Kingdoms Period led the army on a southern expedition, he subdued the chief Long Youna in Yunnan, and bestowed the surname of Zhang on him, so he was also known as Zhang Long Youna. In the Tang Dynasty, Tribe Xi was conferred by the emperor with the surname of Zhang. As an ancient tribe in northern China, Tribe Xi dated back to the Shang and Zhou dynasties. It met its demise in the Jin Dynasty (1115-1234).

Originating from changed surnames: During the Three Kingdom Period, the famous general of State Wei, Zhang Liao was originally surnamed Nie before he changed it to Zhang in order to avoid conflict. His descendants thereby established Zhang as their surname.

In addition, there have also been some ethnic groups who changed their surnames to Han's surnames in the process of interaction and communication. Some of the ethnic groups such as Achang, Naxi, Lisu, Yao, Zhuang, Li, Gaoshan, Tibetans and others also changed their surnames to Zhang.

张仲景雕像（图片提供：微图）
Sculpture of Zhang Zhongjing

Famous Personages Surnamed Zhang in History

Zhang Zhongjing was a famous medical scientist in the late Eastern Han Dynasty. He gathered a wide variety of prescriptions, established the principle of Syndrome Differentiation of the Six Meridians, and also authored the masterpiece *Treatise on Febrile and Miscellaneous Diseases*, making him praised as the Sage of Medicine. The Syndrome Differentiation of the Six Meridians that he established set a precedent for syndrome differentiation and treatment, and formed a unique system of Chinese medical ideas, which has become the basic clinic principles for traditional Chinese medicine. In addition to the feature of integrating theory, methodology, prescriptions and medicines, *Treatise on Febrile and Miscellaneous Diseases* also expounded the author's excellent thoughts about, "Treating the illness of family members and such high offices as kings in the upper level, saving the poor and low-status people from difficulties in the lower level, and maintaining the full physical growth and nurturing for oneself in the intermediary level." It has been highly regarded by doctors of all generations.

八卦中为乾卦；"丰"则是"三"字中间有一竖，代表阴，为坤卦。"三丰"即含有乾坤合一、阴阳变化之意。张三丰是武当派的创始人，开创了武当拳等道教武术。其著述甚丰，有《大道论》《玄机直讲》《玄要篇》等，其中不少篇章为后代奉道者所推崇。千百年来，由于道教理论玄奥、文字晦涩，不

• 湖北武当山上的紫霄宫

紫霄宫始建于明永乐十一年（1413年），是武当山上著名的道观。

Purple Cloud Palace at Wudang Mountain, Hubei Province

Established in the 11th year of the Yongle Period (1413) in the Ming Dynasty (1368-1644), the Purple Cloud Palace is a famous Taoist temple in Wudang Mountain.

能为社会所广泛接受，其传播受到了阻碍。张三丰则采用歌词的体裁和通俗的文字把玄奥的道教理论化为通俗易懂的丹词——《无根树》。

Zhang Sanfeng was an important figure of Taoism. Zhang Sanfeng's original given name was Quanyi, or Junbao, and title name Xuanxuanzi. The character of *San* ("三 " meaning three) in his given name represents *Yang*, which corresponds to the Heaven diagram in the Eight Diagrams, while the other character of *Feng* ("丰" meaning abundance) is formed by having a vertical line going across the three lines in the character of *San*, which represents

张三丰像
Portrait of Zhang Sanfeng

Yin and corresponds to the Earth diagram. Therefore, the name Sanfeng implies the concept of the integration of Heaven and Earth as well as the interaction between *Yin* and *Yang*. Zhang Sanfeng was the founder of the Wudang School, and the creator of the Taoist martial arts of Wudang boxing, and others. He also left many writings, such as the *Theory of the Grand Dao*, *Straight Explanation of the Profound Mysteries* and *Discourse on the Profundity*. Among them, many chapters have been highly regarded by later generations of Taoists. For thousands of years, Taoist theories and writings have never been widely accepted by the general public because of their obscurity and mystics. Nevertheless, Zhang Sanfeng was still able to make use of the genre of lyrical texts coupled with vernacular language to render Taoist theories in accessible terms in *Rootless Tree*.

名门望族

　　名门望族指高贵的、地位显赫的家庭或有特权的家族。在所有的名门望族中，最为突出的就是各朝代的统治者，即皇族。自秦代至清代，中国处于封建社会时期，每个朝代的统治者都采用世袭制将统治权一代一代地传下去，不遇到特殊情况，是不会中断的。作为社会的最高等级，皇族的姓氏成为当时最为显赫、尊贵的标志，例如汉代的刘姓、唐代的李姓、宋代的赵姓、明代的朱姓等。

　　春秋末年，孔子创立了儒家学派，被尊为"孔圣人"。他提出了崇尚礼乐和仁义，提倡忠恕和中庸之道，主张德治、仁政，重视伦常关系的思想学说。自汉武帝时开始，儒家学说受到统治阶级的推崇，成为中国人世代秉承的文化思想。孔姓被称为"儒家第一姓"，孔氏家族成为中国历史上具有影响力的名门望族。

　　山西太原的王氏家族从魏晋到唐代都十分显赫，自古有"天下王氏出太原"的说法。东晋书法家王羲之、唐代诗人王维等都是太原王氏的后裔。

Prominent Families and Prestigious Clans

Prominent families and prestigious clans refer to the noble, prominent, or privileged families. The most distinguished among all prominent families and prestigious clans are the ruling class in each dynasty, the imperial family. During the reign of feudal society in China from the Qin Dynasty to the Qing Dynasty, the rulers of each dynasty utilized the hereditary system to keep the authoritarian rule of feudalism within the families for generation after generation. Unless there were special circumstances, this lineage would not be interrupted. As the top-class of society at the time, the surnames of the imperial families became the most prominent and distinguished symbols, such as the surname of Liu in the Han Dynasty, that of Li in the Tang Dynasty, Zhao in the Song Dynasty, Zhu in the Ming Dynasty, and so forth.

During the late Spring and Autumn Period, Confucius founded the Confucian School and was revered as the Saint of Kong. He upheld the ideas of rites, music, kindheartedness and righteousness, advocated for loyalty, forgiveness, and the doctrine of the golden mean, and proposed governing by virtues and policy of benevolence, with great emphasis attached to the ideology and doctrine of ethical family relations. Since the reign of Emperor Wu of Han Dynasty, Confucianism was highly advocated by the ruling class and has become the cultural ideology upheld by the Chinese people. After Confucius, the Kong family has been referred to as the first surname of Confucianism, and has become the most influential family and prestigious clan in Chinese history.

The clan of Wang in Taiyuan of Shanxi Province is a prominent noble heritage from the Three Kingdoms Period and Jin Dynasty to the Tang Dynasty. Since ancient times, there has been a saying that, "All Wangs originated from Taiyuan." Calligrapher Wang Xizhi from the Eastern Jin Dynasty, the poet Wang Wei in the Tang Dynasty and many others were descendants of the clan of Wang in Taiyuan.

王家大院
王家大院地处山西太原灵石县，是太原王氏后裔于清代初期开始修建的一处城堡式建筑，风格古朴，有"中国民居艺术馆"的美誉。

Wang's Grand Courtyard
Located in Lingshi County of Taiyuan City, Shanxi Province, the Wang's Grand Courtyard is a castle-like building that was constructed by the descendants of the clan of Wang of Taiyuan in the early Qing Dynasty. Characterized by a plain rustic style, the Wang's Grand Courtyard enjoys the reputation of the Chinese Folk House's Museum.

刘姓

目前，刘姓人口在中国姓氏中排第四。

刘姓是中国历史上最为强盛的朝代之一——汉代的皇姓，汉朝的首位皇帝为汉高祖刘邦。历史上的皇帝中，刘姓的最多。晋代末年，为躲避战争，刘姓族人开始南迁。宋代和明代，刘姓人口主要分布在河北、山东、江西等地。如今，刘姓人口主要分布在河南、河北、山东、黑龙江、辽宁、四川、安徽、湖南、湖北等地。

姓氏起源

刘姓的源头主要有三个：一是出自伊祁姓，二是出自姬姓，三是出自皇帝赐姓或改姓。

出自伊祁姓。尧是上古时期的部落联盟首领，因出生在伊祁山，

Liu

At present, the surname of Liu ranks fourth in terms of population.

The surname of Liu is the imperial surname of one of the most powerful dynasties in China's history, the Han Dynasty, founded by the forefather Liu Bang, Emperor Gaozu of Han. The most surname for emperors in history is Liu. At the end of the Jin Dynasty (265-420), the Liu clansmen began to travel south in order to escape the war. During the Song Dynasty and Ming Dynasty, the population with the surname of Liu was primarily distributed across Hebei, Shandong and Jiangxi. Today, the population with the surname of

- 汉高祖刘邦像

刘邦是汉代的开国皇帝，也是第一位刘姓皇帝。

Portrait of Liu Bang, Emperor Gaozu of the Han Dynasty (206 B.C.-220 A.D.)

Liu Bang was the founding emperor of the Han Dynasty, also the first emperor with the surname of Liu.

● 尧帝像
Portrait of Emperor Yao

以地名为姓，始为伊祁姓。尧将第九个儿子源明赐封在刘国（今河北唐县），刘国灭亡后，其后世子孙以国名为姓，始为刘姓。

出自姬姓。东周时期，周定王赐弟弟姬季子封地刘邑，其后代便以封地为姓。

出自皇帝赐姓或改姓。秦代末年，各地相继有人起义反抗暴秦，刘邦和项羽就是其中最为杰出的代表。刘邦最终打败了项羽，建立了汉王朝。为感谢项羽

Liu is located mainly in Henan, Hebei, Shandong, Heilongjiang, Liaoning, Sichuan, Anhui, Hunan and Hubei.

Origin of Liu

There are three main origins for the surname of Liu. The first is from the surname Yiqi, the second is from the surname of Ji, and the third is a surname conferred by the emperor or a changed surname.

Originated from the surname of Yiqi: Yao was a leader of the tribal alliance in ancient times. Born in Yiqi Mountain, Yao was surnamed after the mountain as the initiator of the Yiqis. Yao conferred his ninth son, Yuan Ming, with the State of Liu (now Tang County in Hebei). After the fall of the Liu State, the descendants took on the nation's name as their surname, and thus began the surname Liu.

Originated from the surname Ji: During the Eastern Zhou Dynasty, King Ding of Zhou bestowed the manor of Liu upon his brother Ji Jizi. Since then, his descendants took the manor as their surname.

Originated from an emperor's conferment or a changed surname: During the late Qin Dynasty, people in various areas revolted against the tyrannical

的叔叔项伯在鸿门宴上的帮助，便赐项伯刘姓，并世代相传。

少数民族在与汉族融合的过程中，出现了很多汉化的现象，少数民族中的一些人便改姓刘。

Qin Dynasty in succession. Among them, Liu Bang and Xiang Yu were the most outstanding. Liu Bang eventually defeated Xiang Yu and established the Han Dynasty. In order to show gratitude for the help of Xiang Yu's uncle, Xiang Bo in the Hongmen Banquet, Liu Bang conferred the imperial surname on Xiang Bo, which was passed down from generation to generation.

In the process of the interaction and communication with the Han people, some ethnic groups converted their surnames into Han surnames. Liu was one of these surnames.

Famous Personages Surnamed Liu in History

Liu Bang (256 B.C.-195 B.C.), name Ji, was the founding emperor of the Western Han Dynasty. He was an outstanding statesman and strategist in Chinese history. At first, Liu Bang was a minor official in the Qin Dynasty. During the first year of the reign of Second Emperor of Qin Dynasty when Chen Sheng and Wu Guang waged their uprisings in the township of Daze, Liu Bang gathered hundreds of people and slew the magistrate

- 鸿门宴壁画（汉）

Mural of Hongmen Banquet (Han Dynasty, 206 B.C.-220 A.D.)

刘姓历史名人

刘邦（前256—前195），本名季，西汉开国皇帝，中国历史上杰出的政治家、战略家。刘邦初为秦朝的小官。秦二世元年（前209年），陈胜、吴广在大泽乡起义后，刘邦聚合数百人，杀死县官，起兵响应。刘邦曾一度归属项梁。项梁战死后，刘邦与项梁的侄子项羽继续坚持反秦斗争。后来，刘邦为了与西楚霸王项羽争夺政权而进行了一场大规模的楚汉战争。刘邦在击败项羽后统一了天下，建立了汉朝，于公元前202年登基称帝，建都长安（今陕西西安）。刘邦登基后，先后消灭了异姓王侯的割据势力，加强了中央集权，并且建章立制，采用休养生息的宽松政策治理天下，不但安抚了人民，还迅速恢复了生产，发展了经济。

刘禹锡（772—842），唐代文学家、诗人，有"诗豪"之称。刘禹锡性格刚毅，极富豪猛之气。他的诗，无论是短章还是长篇，大都简洁、明快，既蕴含哲人的睿智，又富有诗人的挚情。他的咏史诗尤为著名，表达了深深的感慨。《乌

to join the revolt. Liu Bang was affiliated to Xiang Liang. After Xiang Liang was killed in the battlefield, Liu Bang and Xiang Liang's nephew Xiang Yu carried on the revolt against Qin. Later, in order to compete for the political power against Xiang Yu, the King of Western Chu, Liu Bang waged a large-scale war known as Chu-Han Contention. After defeating Xiang Yu, Liu Bang unified the country and established the Han Dynasty. He ascended to the throne in 202 B.C., and established the capital in Chang'an (now Xi'an, Shaanxi Province). After his ascension, Liu Bang successively eliminated the separatist forces of feudal kings and vassals with different surnames, consolidated the centralization of state power, established systems and institutions, and adopted a loose policy for recuperation. This not only appeased the people, but also quickly restored production and furthered the development of the economy.

Liu Yuxi (772-842) was a famous literary writer and poet in the Tang Dynasty, known as the Poet Master. Liu Yuxi was stout and resolute with an air of straight forwardness and fieriness. His poems, long or short, were mostly simple and neat, tinged with the wisdom

衣巷》就是他的代表作："朱雀桥边野草花，乌衣巷口夕阳斜。旧时王谢堂前燕，飞入寻常百姓家。"这首诗采取以小见大的手法来描写王公贵族的盛衰变化，后面的两句更是被千古传诵。

of a philosopher and the deep feelings of a poet. He was particularly famed for his historical poems, which expressed his deep emotions. Among them, *Wuyi Lane* stands out as his masterpiece, "Wild flowers growing by the Rosefinch Bridge, the sun setting low at the corner of Wuyi Lane; Sparrows nestled at the Wang's and the Xie's mansions, now fly to the commoners' houses." The poem adopts the metonymic approach to describe the rise and fall of noble families. The last couplet of the poem has been read through all ages.

- 刘禹锡像
Portrait of Liu Yuxi

陈姓

目前，陈姓人口在中国姓氏中排第五。

唐宋时期，陈姓族人就已经开始南迁，到达广东、福建等

Chen

Presently, Chen is ranked the fifth among Chinese surnames in terms of population.

During the Tang and Song dynasties, the Chen's clansmen had already begun to migrate south to Guangdong, Fujian, and

地。明清时期，陈姓已经遍布全国各地。如今，陈姓主要分布在河南、山东、山西、江苏、浙江、广东、福建等地。在香港、澳门、台湾等地区，陈姓人口的比重相当大。

姓氏起源

陈姓的源头主要有两个：一是出自姚姓，二是出自赐姓或改姓。

舜帝像
Portrait of Emperor Shun

other provinces. By the Ming and Qing dynasties, the Chens had already spread across the country. Today, the population with the surname of Chen is primarily distributed across Henan, Shandong, Shanxi, Jiangsu, Zhejiang, Guangdong and Fujian. The Chens make up a significant proportion of the population especially in Hong Kong, Macao and Taiwan.

Origin of Chen

There are two main origins for the surname of Chen: One is from the surname of Yao, and the other is from either a conferred surname or a changed surname.

Originating from the surname of Yao: Shun is the eighth-generation descendant of Huangdi in legend, who inherited Yao's throne and became the leader of the tribal alliance. Born in the land of Yao, he took the name of the location as his surname and began the Yao clan. Later on, a part of the tribe relocated to the bank of Gui River; therefore, adopted Gui as their surname. After King Wu of Zhou overthrew the Shang Dynasty and established the Zhou Dynasty, he regarded Shun's descendant, Guiman, as the offspring of a sage and conferred Marquis of Chen on Guiman

出自姚姓。传说中，舜是黄帝的八世孙，继承尧的帝位当了部落联盟的首领。舜出生在姚地，以地名为姓，始为姚姓。之后，一部分族人迁居至妫水，因此便以"妫"为姓。周武王推翻商朝建立周朝后，将舜的后裔妫满视为圣人的后代，封他为陈侯，赐陈地（今河南淮阳）。妫满在陈地建立了陈with the manor at Chen (now Huaiyang County, Henan Province). After Guiman established the State of Chen in the land of Chen, his descendants began to adopt the name of the land as their surname.

Originating from a conferred surname and a changed surname: In the late Yuan Dynasty, Zhu Yuanzhang (1328-1398) launched the peasant uprising against the dynasty. After defeating other uprising forces in 1368, he established a new regime in Nanjing called Ming. A number of Mongolian nobilities of the Yuan Dynasty surrendered to the Ming Dynasty and were conferred with the Han surname of Chen.

In the process of interaction and communication with Han people, such ethnic groups as the Zhuang, Li, Yi, Koreans, Bai, Gaoshan, Hui, She and other ethnic groups also gradually changed to Han surnames, and Chen is one of these surnames.

Famous Personages Surnamed Chen in History

Chen Shubao (553-604), also known as the Final Lord of Chen, was the last emperor of the State of Chen during the Southern and Northern dynasties. During his reign, Chen Shubao indulged in

陈叔宝像
Portrait of Chen Shubao

国，他的后世子孙便以国为姓，始为陈姓。

出自赐姓或改姓。元代末年，朱元璋（1328—1398）等人发动农民起义反抗元王朝，并于1368年击败其他起义部队，在今南京建立了新政权，国号"明"。一些元朝的蒙古贵族投降明朝后，朱元璋赐他们汉姓陈。

壮族、黎族、彝族、朝鲜族、白族、高山族、回族、畲族等少数民族在与汉族融合的过程中，逐渐改为汉族姓氏，陈姓便是其中之一。

陈姓历史名人

陈叔宝（553—604）又称"陈后主"，是南北朝时期南朝陈政权的最后一个皇帝。陈叔宝当政期间贪恋美色、铺张浪费、荒废朝政，使得国家逐渐衰败。公元581年，杨坚建立了隋朝，史称"隋文帝"，开启了统一全国的军事行动。公元589年，隋朝派军队进攻陈的都城建康（今江苏南京），陈叔宝认为有长江这一天然屏障，完全能够阻断隋朝军队的进攻，因而并未理会。同年，都城建康失守，陈政权灭

luxury, waste and extravagance, leaving political affairs unattended and bringing the nation to decline. In 581, when Yang Jian established the Sui Dynasty (581-618), he became Emperor Wen of Sui and launched military activities to unify the country. In 589, the government of the Sui Dynasty dispatched troops to attack the capital city of State of Chen, Jiankang (now Nanjing, Jiangsu Province). Chen Shubao ignored the threat because he believed that the Yangtze River would serve as a natural barrier to completely block the Sui army's invasion. In the same year, the capital of Jiankang was seized, the State of Chen fell, and Chen Shubao became a stateless monarch. However, Chen Shubao was very accomplished in poetry, especially which in the poetic forms of five-character lines and seven-character lines, his most famous work being the seven-character poem *Back Courtyard Flowers on Jade Trees*.

Chen Hongshou (1599-1652), with the title names of Old Lotus, was a famous painter, calligrapher and poet in the late Ming Dynasty and early Qing Dynasty. Chen Hongshou specialized in painting personages, flowers, birds and landscapes, among which his portrait paintings had the greatest influence on

亡，陈叔宝成了亡国之君。然而，陈叔宝在诗文方面卓有成就，尤其擅长五言诗、七言诗，最著名的作品是七言诗《玉树后庭花》。

陈洪绶（1599—1652），号老莲，是明末清初著名的画家、书法家、诗人。陈洪绶擅画人物、花

future generations. He is considered as a significant painter who inherited the ancient traditions and began the new style of modern portrait painting. His portrait of Qu Yuan (famous Chinese statesman and poet in the Warring States Period) has been regarded as a classic masterpiece that no one can surpass up to now. His illustrations for portraits, such as *Nine Songs*, *Romance of the West Chamber*, *Leaves of Water Margin Heroes* and *Leaves of Encyclopedic Past* were all engraved into prints by

- 《玉树后庭花》（明）（图片提供：FOTOE）

陈叔宝经常在宫中与嫔妃、女学士宴饮，相互赋诗赠答，并命人谱曲演唱。《玉树后庭花》全文："丽宇芳林对高阁，新装艳质本倾城。映户凝娇乍不进，出帷含态笑相迎。妖姬脸似花含露，玉树流光照后庭。"

Back Courtyard Flowers on Jade Trees
(Ming Dynasty, 1368-1644)

Chen Shubao often had feasts and drinks with his concubines and female scholars in the palace. They would compose lyric poems to each other and order the poems to be tuned for songs. The full text of *Back Courtyard Flowers on Jade Trees* goes, "Splendid roofs and blooming woods are facing towering pavilions; beauty clad in new makeup can topple the towers. The sudden pause of her charming shadow is reflected on the door, while the smile unveiled bears a welcome air. The pretty face is like a flower rinsed in dew while the flowing light among jade trees light up the back courtyard."

鸟、山水，尤以人物画对后世影响最大，是一位继承古代传统、开启近代人物画新风的重要画家。他创作的屈原像至今无人能超越，被奉为屈原像的经典。陈洪绶所绘的绣像插图《九歌》《西厢记》《水浒叶子》《博古叶子》等均由名工镌刻成版画，付梓刊行，对中国版画艺术的发展具有重要的意义。

famous workers for publication. They have been of great significance in the development of Chinese engraving art.

- 《对镜仕女图》

陈洪绶画中的仕女装束十分古雅，端庄中又透着一丝妩媚。

Portrait of A Lady Facing A Mirror

The lady in Chen Hongshou's painting is dressed in very quaint attire, with a dignified expression and a trace of charm.

- 陈洪绶像

Portrait of Chen Hongshou

《水浒叶子》

《水浒叶子》是陈洪绶参考民间流行的马吊牌绘制而成的。"叶子"即纸牌，是现代扑克牌的雏形，因最初只有树叶一样的大小，故名。在古代，叶子是博戏（赌输赢、胜负的游戏）用具，也可作为行酒令（酒席上的助兴游戏）用具。《水浒叶子》中的人物以明初小说《水浒传》中的人物为原型，共四十幅，栩栩如生地刻画出了宋江等水浒英雄。作者大量运用方笔直拐的画法进行勾画，线条简单，但变化十分强烈，恰到好处地运用衣纹的走向表现出人物的动势。这套图一经出版，民间争相购买，文人、画友也交口称赞，以至于后世绘写水浒英雄的画家很难超越他。

- 《博古叶子·百里奚》

《博古叶子》为陈洪绶所绘，明末徽派著名刻工黄建中所刻，共四十八幅。黄建中的精湛技艺与陈洪绶的设计堪称珠联璧合。百里奚是春秋时期著名的政治家，晚年在秦国任大夫，帮助秦穆公成为春秋五霸之一。

Leaves of Ancient Sages: Baili Xi

Leaves of Ancient Sages was drawn by Chen Hongshou and carved by Huang Jianzhong, a famous Hui-style engraver from the late Ming Dynasty. *Leaves of Ancient Sages* consisted of 48 illustrations. Huang Jianzhong's superb skills and Chen Hongshou's design was a perfect match for the masterpiece. Baili Xi was a famous statesman during the Spring and Autumn Period. In his later years, he became a minister in the State of Qin and assisted Duke Mu of Qin to develop the Qin State into one of the five major powers during the Spring and Autumn Period.

Leaves of the Marshes' Heroes

Leaves of the Marshes' Heroes were drawn by Chen Hongshou with references to the popular *Madiao* cards at the time. The leaves were made of paper cards, a prototype of modern poker cards, about the size of leaves, hence the name. In the ancient times, leaves were tools used in gambling (games of win or loss), or used as utensils in drinking wager games (entertaining game during a banquet). The pictures on these leaves, totaling forty in number, were based on the character from the novel *Heroes of the Marshes* from the early Ming Dynasty. They provided vivid pictures of such heroes as Song Jiang and others in the novel. The painter made massive use of straight-angled brushwork to trace the figures in simple yet powerfully changeable lines, and skillfully utilize the direction of the wrinkling lines on the character's clothing to display the active momentum of the characters. When this set of illustrations were published, they were so popularly purchased by local people and so greatly praised by fellow-painters that any paintings of the novel done in later generations could not surpass them.

- 《水浒叶子·武松》

此图上面书写着"八万贯",左侧书写着"行者武松申大义斩嫂头啾啾鬼哭鸳鸯楼"。讲述的是武松的嫂子与他人通奸,并合谋将其哥哥武大郎杀害,他发现后斩下了嫂子的头为哥哥报仇的故事。在民间,武松被认为是快意恩仇、伸张正义的英雄。

Leaves of the Marshes' Heroes: Wu Song

The writing above says: 80,000 *Guan* (monetary unit used in ancient China), while the writing to the left side of the book says: the traveler Wu Song chopped off his sister-in-law's head to serve justice while ghostly cries sound throughout the Mandarin Duck Hall. It tells the story that after Wu Song found out his adulterous sister-in-law murdered his brother, he sought revenge by beheading her. Among the masses, Wu Song has been taken as a hero who clearly distinguishes kindness and hatred, and serves justice.

杨姓

目前，杨姓人口在中国姓氏中排第六。

杨姓发源于晋地（今山西），随后不断向各地迁移。战国末期，杨姓族人在长江中下游地区都有分布。魏晋南北朝时期政局动荡，战火不断，杨姓族人向长江以南地区迁移。在明代初年山西洪洞大槐树的人口大迁移中，杨姓族人是主要的迁民，被分迁到江苏、浙江、云南等地。如今，杨姓主要分布在四川、河南、云南、山东、湖北、湖南等地。

姓氏起源

杨姓主要出自西周时期的姬姓，不过关于其得姓始祖的说法有所不同，一说是周宣王的儿子长父，一说是春秋时期晋武公的次子伯侨。

周宣王四十二年（前786年），周宣王赏赐儿子长父封邑杨地，并让他建立诸侯国杨国，人们称他为"杨侯"。2003年在陕西眉县杨家村出土的"四十二年逨鼎"上的铭文记述了这一历史事实。长父的后人以封地为姓，始为杨姓。

Yang

At present, Yang is ranked sixth among Chinese surnames in terms of population.

The surname of Yang originated from the land of Jin (now Shanxi Province), and continued to move to various regions. In the late Warring States Period, the Yang clan was distributed along the middle and lower reaches of the Yangtze River. During the Wei, Jin, Southern and Northern dynasties, the Yang clansmen started migrating to the southern regions of the Yangtze River due to political instability and the ongoing war. During the Great Migration of the Great Pagoda Tree of Hongtong in Shanxi Province in the early years of the Ming Dynasty, the Yangs were among the major migrants and relocated to Jiangsu, Zhejiang, Yunnan and other provinces. Today, the population with the surname of Yang is mainly distributed across Sichuan, Henan, Yunnan, Shandong, Hubei and Hunan.

Origin of Yang

The surname of Yang primarily originated from the surname of Ji in the Western Zhou Dynasty. However, there are different theories as to where it came from. One theory argues that it derived

• 四十二年逨鼎（西周）

四十二年逨鼎上铸有280个字，记载了逨受周王命辅佐长父建立杨国，以及他因征伐北方游牧民族有功，而受到周王册封和赏赐的历史。

Forty-second Year's *Lai Ding* (Western Zhou Dynasty, 1046 B.C.-771 B.C.)

The casting of the Forty-second Year's *Lai Ding* (*Ding*, an ancient cooking vessel) contains 280 characters which documented how Lai was ordered by the King of Zhou to assist Chang Fu in establishing the State of Yang, and how Chang Fu was praised and rewarded by the King of Zhou for his meritorious services in conquering the northern nomad tribe.

另一说是周成王赐予其弟姬虞封邑唐地（今山西翼城县西），因唐地临靠晋水，便以"晋"为国号。姬虞即春秋时期诸侯国晋国的始祖。晋武公时，晋国歼灭了包括杨国在内的一些周边小国，并将之赐封给次子姬伯侨，封姬伯侨为杨侯。姬伯侨的后人便以杨为姓。

from the son of King Xuan of Zhou by the name of Chang Fu. The other theory proposes that it was from the second son of Duke Wu of State Jin, Boqiao, in the Spring and Autumn Period.

In the forty-second year (786 B.C.) of the King Xuan's reign in the Zhou Period, King Xuan of Zhou bestowed his son, Chang Fu, with the land of Yang, where Chang Fu subsequently established the Vassal State of Yang and became known as Marquis of Yang. This historical fact is recorded in the inscriptions on the Forty-second Year's *Lai Ding* (*Ding*, an ancient cooking vessel) unearthed in 2003 from Yang's Village at the County of Mei in Shaanxi Province. Descendants of Chang Fu later took on the name of the land as their surname, hence the surname Yang.

Another theory proposes that King Cheng of Zhou bestowed the land of Tang (west of current Yicheng County in Shanxi Province) upon his brother Ji Yu. Since the land of Tang was close to River Jin, Jin was adopted as the national title. Therefore, Ji Yu became the father of the Vassal State of Jin. During the reign of Duke Wu, the State of Jin annihilated some smaller nearby states, including the State Yang, which was given to his second son Ji Boqiao, dubbed as the

杨姓历史名人

杨坚（541—604），隋王朝的开国皇帝，即隋文帝。隋文帝定都长安（今陕西西安），结束了魏晋南北朝时期近四百年的南北分裂的局面。他推行了一系列的政策：在中央实行三省六部制，将地方的州、郡、县三级制改为州、县两级制，地方官吏由中央任免，以此来巩固中央集权；推行均田制，使无地的农民获得了荒地，进行开垦、种植；整顿户籍，实行了"大索貌

- 隋文帝杨坚像

Portrait of Emperor Wen of Sui, Yang Jian

Marquis of Yang. The later generations took on the name of the land and changed their surname to Yang.

Famous Personages Surnamed Yang in History

Yang Jian (541-604), known in history as Emperor Wen of Sui, was the founding emperor of the Sui Dynasty, who established the imperial capital in Chang'an (now Xi'an City in Shaanxi Province) and ended nearly four hundred years of the north-south separation status from the Wei, Jin, Southern and Northern dynasties. Emperor Wen of Sui also implemented a series of policies. The Three Councils and Six Ministries System was set up in the central government, and the three-level system of *Zhou* (country divisions), prefectures and counties was changed to the two-tier system of *Zhou* and counties. Local officials were to be appointed and removed by the central government as a means to consolidate the centralized state power. He implemented the land equalization policy so that landless peasants were entitled to wasteland for cultivation, rectified household registration, and enforced the Great Feature Reading Index, which required officials to check the census based on facial appearances, all these

阅"法，要求官吏根据相貌来检查户口，由此增加了国家的赋税收入；崇尚节俭，推行节俭政策，减轻农民徭役、苛捐负担；修改法律和制度，废除了隋代之前历朝、历代沿袭的宫刑、车裂等酷刑。隋文帝在位期间民生富庶，政治安定。他开创了"开皇之治"，使得当时的中国成为盛世之国。

杨玉环（719—756），号太真，是唐玄宗李隆基的贵妃，古代四大美人之一。传说，有一天杨玉环在宫苑里赏花，无意间碰到了含羞草，含羞草的花瓣立即收缩，叶子也卷了起来。宫女看到后便说杨玉环的美貌让花都自惭形秽，羞得躲了起来。于是，杨玉环便有了"羞花"的美名。许多文学作品中都有关于她的描写，如唐代著名文学家白居易在其诗作《长恨歌》中所写的"回眸一笑百媚生，六宫粉黛无颜色"，诗人杜牧的诗作《过华清宫》中的"一骑红尘妃子笑，无人知是荔枝来"，李白诗作《清平调》中所写的"名花倾国两相欢，长得君王带笑看"等。《贵妃醉酒》就是以杨贵妃为主要人物的经典京剧剧目。

thereby increasing taxation. Emperor Wen of Sui also advocated for frugality and carried out a frugality policy. He reduced farmers' compulsory labor services and burden of taxation, modified the legal system and abolished cruel torture punishments such as castration and dismemberment, which were practiced in previous dynasties prior to the Sui Dynasty. During his reign, people lived an abundant life, and the society was stable, having thus created the Liberal Rule of the Emperor and making China at that time a country of prosperity.

Yang Yuhuan (719-756), courtesy name Taizhen, was the highest-ranking imperial concubine to Emperor Xuanzong of Tang, Li Longji. She was one of the four great beauties in ancient times. According to legends, one day when Yang Yuhuan was enjoying the flowers in the palace garden, she inadvertently touched a mimosa and the flower petals immediately shrunk and the leaves rolled up. Upon seeing this, the palace maids drew the comparison that Yang Yuhuan was so beautiful that even flowers would shy away in shame. Since then, Yang Yuhuan was given the reputation as the Flower-shyer. There have been numerous descriptions of her in literary works. In his poem the *Song of Everlasting Sorrow*, Bai Juyi, a famous Tang Dynasty poet, wrote, "A hundred of charm given off from her one smile, and all the well-dressed palace ladies became colorless." Du Mu, a Tang Dynasty poet, wrote in his poem *Passing Huaqing Palace* that, "The imperial concubine gave a tacit smile on seeing the trace of the horseman coming from far away, while no one knew it was but delivering her favorite fruit of litchi." Li Bai also wrote in his poem *Tune of Serenity*, "As a beautiful flower feasting for eyes; She attracts the king's gaze in smiles." Yang Yuhuan is also a featured character in the classic Chinese opera, *The Drunken Beauty*.

- 《华清出浴图》（清·康涛）
  此图画的是杨贵妃在皇家行宫华清宫沐浴后出来的情景。

Portrait of Bathing Beauty Yang Yuhuan in Huaqing Palace, by Kang Tao (Qing Dynasty, 1616-1911)

This picture describes the scene of the imperial concubine Yang Yuhuan coming out of the bath in Huaqing Palace, an imperial resort palace.

《贵妃醉酒》

　　《贵妃醉酒》是京剧经典剧目，最早出现在清乾隆年间。该剧主要讲述的是唐玄宗与杨贵妃相约至百花亭赏花、饮酒，当杨贵妃到达百花亭准备好宴席后却迟迟没能等到唐玄宗，原来唐玄宗已改去其他皇妃宫中。心生怨恨的杨贵妃命高力士、裴力士两位宦官在一旁伺候，独自饮起酒来。借酒浇愁愁更愁，她逐渐显出醉态。京剧大师梅兰芳对该剧目进行了细致的打磨，用杨贵妃三次饮酒时身体姿态的不同表现其失落、懊恼、嫉恨的心绪。

- **《贵妃醉酒》京剧剧照**
  此为梅兰芳演唱《贵妃醉酒》时的剧照。梅兰芳是中国京剧四大名旦之首，梅派创始人。《贵妃醉酒》是梅兰芳的代表作品，其中衔杯、卧鱼、醉步、扇舞等动作优美而自然，难度颇高。
  Stage Photo of *The Drunken Beauty*
  It is the stage photo of *The Drunken Beauty* performed by Mei Lanfang. Mei Lanfang ranks first in the four famous Dan's role (female role) performers, and was the founder of the Mei-style. *The Drunken Beauty* is Mei Lanfang's representative work. Highly difficult stage moves including taking the cup between lips, lying like a fish, drunken steps and fan dance were performed gracefully and naturally by him.

The Drunken Beauty

The Drunken Beauty is a classic Peking Opera that premiered during the reign of Emperor Qianlong in the Qing Dynasty. The story of the opera focuses on the planned meeting of Emperor Xuanzong of Tang and Yang Yuhuan to drink at Hundred-flower Pavilion. When imperial concubine Yang arrived at the pavilion and had already prepared a feast, Emperor Xuanzong of Tang did not show up. Instead, the emperor headed to the chamber of another concubine. Bitterly, Yang Yuhuan ordered the two eunuchs, Gao Lishi and Pei Lishi, to wait by her side as she drank alone. The more she drank to quench her sorrow, the more sorrow she felt, and she gradually became tipsy. Peking Opera master Mei Lanfang carefully analyzed the story of this play and made delicate changes in Yang Yuhuan's physical behavior during her three drinking scenes so as to express her feelings of loss, annoyance and envy.

赵姓

目前，赵姓人口在中国姓氏中排第七。

最初，赵姓族人多聚居在甘肃天水、河南颍川等地。西汉时期，赵姓族人迁居至瀛洲（今河北河间）。南朝时期，天水的赵姓一支迁居长江以南。宋代是赵姓王朝，赵姓族人在中国各地都有分布。在明代初年山西洪洞大槐树的人口大迁移中，赵姓族人是主要的迁民，

Zhao

At present, the surname Zhao is ranked the seventh among Chinese surnames in terms of population.

At first, the majority of the Zhao clan settled in Tianshui of Gansu Province and Yingchuan of Henan Province. During the Western Han Dynasty, the Zhaos moved to Yingzhou (now Hejian, Hebei Province). During the Southern dynasties, the Zhao clan in Tianshui relocated to the south of the Yangtze River. Zhao was the

被分迁至河北、河南、浙江、福建、广东、四川等地。清朝末年，"闯关东"之风流行，中原人口纷纷前往东北地区开荒，赵姓人口也在迁移队伍中。如今，赵姓人口主要分布在山东、河南、河北、黑龙江、江苏等地。

姓氏起源

赵姓的源头主要有两个：一是出自嬴姓，二是出自赐姓。

出自嬴姓。周穆王时，有一位名为造父的驾车大夫，是嬴姓始祖伯益的后代。《史记》记载："穆王使造父御，西巡狩，见西王母，乐之忘归。而徐偃王反，穆王日驰千里马，攻徐偃王，大破之。乃赐造父以赵城，由此为赵氏。"传说，造父是西周时期一个擅长驾驭的人，担任驾车大夫官职，他曾将八匹骏马调训好之后献给了周穆王。有一次穆王向西巡守，到了昆仑山西王母处，乐不思归，而这时正好爆发了徐偃王造反，周穆王非常着急。于是造父驾车日驰千里，帮助周穆王及时返回都城镐京平定了叛乱，穆王赐封给他赵城。其后代为纪念祖先，便以封邑为姓，始为赵姓。

imperial surname of the Song Dynasty, and the Zhaos spread across every part of the country. During the Great Migration of the Great Pagoda Tree of Hongtong in Shanxi in the early years of the Ming Dynasty, Zhao was among the major clans of these migrants, who were later relocated in Hebei, Henan, Zhejiang, Fujian, Guangdong, Sichuan and other places. At the end of the Qing Dynasty, there arose a fad to go east of Shanhai Pass, which sent the Central Plains population in flocks to the wastelands of the northeast region, and the Zhao was among this migration wave. Today, the population with the surname of Zhao is distributed across Shandong, Henan, Hebei, Heilongjiang, Jiangsu and other provinces.

Origin of Zhao

There are two main origins for the surname of Zhao. One is from the surname of Ying, and the other is from the conferred surname.

Originated from the surname of Ying: During the reign of King Mu of Zhou, there was a charioteer minister by the name of Zao Fu, who was the descendant of Bo Yi, the ancestor of the Yings. According to the *Historical Records*, "King Mu had Zao Fu drive

出自赐姓。公元960年，赵匡胤开创了大宋王朝，赵姓便成为国姓。宋代君主为封赏有功之臣，便赐予他们国姓"赵"，如北宋时期的西北党项族拓跋部的首领李继捧和李继迁归顺，被赐名为赵保忠和赵保吉。

for his imperial hunting tour to the west, where he met Queen Mother of the West and forgot to return home. On learning that King Yan of Xu rose to rebel, King Mu of Zhou rode on Zao Fu's chariot running thousands of miles back to attack King Yan of Xu and subdued the uprising. King Mu of Zhou subsequently bestowed the City of Zhao to Zao Fu, who later took on the surname of Zhao." The legend has it that Zao Fu was an expert of driving carriages during the Western Zhou Dynasty. He presented eight fine horses that he had tamed to King Mu of Zhou, and took on the official position of charioteer. On an imperial hunting tour to the west, King Mu of Zhou met the Queen Mother of the West at Kunlun Mountains. He was so indulged in the delight that he forgot to return home. It was at this time that the news of the uprising led by King Yan of Xu reached King Mu of Zhou and made him very anxious. In response to the situation, Zao Fu drove the carriage for thousands of miles to transport King Mu of Zhou back to the capital city of Haojing in time to suppress the rebels. King Mu of Zhou subsequently bestowed the City of Zhao to Zao Fu. In commemoration of

- 宋太祖赵匡胤像
  Portrait of Zhao Kuangyin, Emperor Taizu of Song

赵姓历史名人

赵匡胤（927—976），宋朝开国皇帝。赵匡胤原为五代十国时期后周的将领，后在陈桥发动了兵变，身穿象征皇权的黄色龙袍自立为帝，之后建立了统一的王朝宋朝，史称"宋太祖"。他于在位期间加强中央集权，提倡文人政治，推崇儒学，完善科举，奉行以文治国的理念，开创了中国的文治盛世，是一位英明、仁慈、勤政、爱民的皇帝。

• 《浴马图》【局部】（元·赵孟頫）
Bathing Horses, by Zhao Mengfu [Part] (Yuan Dynasty, 1206-1368)

Zao Fu, his descendants took on the name of the bestowed manor as their surname.

Originated from conferred surnames: In 960, Zhao Kuangyin founded the Song Dynasty and established Zhao as the imperial surname. In order to reward those meritorious ministers and officials, the emperor conferred them the imperial surname of Zhao. For instance, when Li Jipeng and Li Jiqian, the Tuoba leaders of the Dangxiang Tribe in the northwest, pledged their allegiance to the Northern Song Dynasty, they were given the names Zhao Baozhong and Zhao Baoji respectively.

Famous Personages Surnamed Zhao in History

Zhao Kuangyin (927-976) was the founding emperor of the Song Dynasty. Formerly a general of Later Zhou (951-960) in the period of Five dynasties and Ten states, Zhao Kuangyin launched a mutiny at Chen Bridge. Draped in the yellow dragon robe, a symbol of the imperial throne, he proclaimed himself as the emperor. He founded the unified Song Dynasty. He was known as the Emperor Taizu of Song. During his reign, the centralized state power was strengthened, literati politicians were promoted, Confucianism was advocated,

赵孟頫（1254—1322），字子昂，号松雪道人，吴兴（今浙江湖州）人，元代著名书画家。他博学多才，在诗文、音乐方面均有造诣，还擅长鉴定古器物，尤其在绘画和书法方面成就最高。他开创了元代新画风，被称为"元人冠冕"。他在书法史上占有重要的地位，是楷书四大家（欧阳询、颜真卿、柳公权、赵孟頫）之一。其传

civil service exams were improved, and the concept of ruling the country by culture was taken. He initiated the golden age of cultural governance in China. Zhao Kuangyin was a wise, benevolent, diligent and caring emperor.

Zhao Mengfu (1254-1322) was courtesy named Zi'ang with the title name of Pine-snow Taoist, a famous calligrapher and painter from Wuxing (now Huzhou, Zhejiang Province) during the Yuan Dynasty. He was knowledgeable and versatile, accomplished in both poetry and music. He was also well-versed in verifying ancient artifacts especially in the fields of painting and calligraphy, with great achievements made. His painting created a new style during the Yuan Dynasty, and he was therefore praised as the Royal Crown of the Yuan. Zhao Mengfu takes up a very important position in the history of Chinese calligraphy. He was one of the four grand masters of regular-script calligraphy (together with Ouyang Xun, Yan Zhenqing and Liu Gongquan). Some of his masterpiece paintings that have been handed down include *Horse Drinking in Countryside During Autumn*, *Autumn Colors on the Que and Hua Mountains* and *Portrait of Arhat in Red*.

- 赵孟頫像
  Portrait of Zhao Mengfu

世绘画代表作有《秋郊饮马图》《鹊华秋色图》《红衣罗汉图》等，书法代表作有《千字文》《胆巴碑》《归去来兮辞》《赤壁赋》《道德经》等，并著有《尚书注》《松雪斋集》。

His masterpieces of calligraphy are typified by *Thousand-Character Classic*, *Danba Stele*, *Returning Home*, *Ode of the Red Cliff* and *Dao De Jing*. He also authored *Notes to the Book of History* and *Collections of Zhao Mengfu*.

赵公元帅

"赵公元帅"就是传说中的赵公明，是专门保佑人们发财的神。赵公明本名朗，字公明。据传说，赵公明是陕西终南山人氏，秦代时为躲避乱世隐居山中，虔诚修行道法。汉代时师从张道陵天师。他骑着黑色的老虎，守护炼丹的丹室。张天师炼丹功成后，将丹药分与赵公明食用，使他获得神力，能够驱雷役电、呼风唤雨。在著名的古典神怪小说《封神演义》中，赵公明获封"玄坛真君"，统"招宝天尊萧升""纳珍天尊曹宝""招财使者陈九公""利市仙官姚少司"四位神仙，专司迎祥纳福、商贾买卖。民间称他为"武财神"，所供神像皆顶盔、披甲、着战袍、执鞭，须黑而浓，十分威猛。神像的周围常有聚宝盆、大元宝之类的物件。

Marshal Zhao Gong

Marshal Zhao Gong refers actually to the legendary Zhao Gongming, the god of wealth in Chinese folklore. Zhao Gongming's given name was Lang, with the title name of Gongming. According to the legend, Zhao Gongming was a native of Zhongnan Mountain in Shaanxi, who secluded himself in the mountains during the troubled times of the Qin Dynasty, and became a devoted practitioner of Taoism. While apprenticing the Heavenly Master, Zhang Daoling in the Han Dynasty, Zhao Gongming was mounting on a black tiger to guard the alchemist chamber where the pill for immortality was made. After the Heavenly Master Zhang successfully made

- 《封神演义》故事年画（清）

  New Year Picture: *Investiture of the Gods* (Qing Dynasty, 1616-1911)

the pill for immortality, he shared it with Zhao Gongming, enabling him to get the divine power to control the thunder and the wind as a result. As depicted in the famous classic fantasy novel *Investiture of the Gods*, Zhao Gongming was given the title of True Lord of Xuantan with the capability to command the four blessing gods: Xiao Sheng, the Heavenly Lord of Treasure Gathering, Cao Bao, the Heavenly Lord of Hoarded Wealth, Chen Jiugong, the Messenger of Wealth, and Yao Shaosi, the Immortal Official of Profits, in order to manage the blessings of good luck and fortune as well as merchants' trading businesses. Zhao Gongming is referred to as the Martial God of Wealth with mighty statues of him with armor, helmets, combat robes, whips in hands and a black thick beard worshipped. Treasure items such as treasure bowls and large gold ingots are often seen around the statues.

黄姓

目前，黄姓人口在中国姓氏中排第八。

秦汉时期，大批黄姓族人迁移到湖北地区，并逐渐向长江以南扩散，在四川、湖南、江西一带都有分布。隋唐时期，黄姓族人的迁移更加频繁，一支从江夏（今湖北云梦县东南）南迁至浙江金华，一支从江夏北迁至蓼城（今河南固始），之后又向南分迁至安徽、江西、福建等地。在明代初年山西洪

- 甲骨文"黄"
  Character of *Huang* in Oracle Bone Script

Huang

At present, Huang is ranked eighth among Chinese surnames in terms of population.

During the Qin and Han dynasties, a large number of the Huang's clansmen migrated to Hubei Province, and gradually spread to the South of the Yangtze River, settling in Sichuan, Hunan and Jiangxi. During the Sui and Tang dynasties, the Huangs migrated even more frequently. One group moved from south of Jiangxia (southeast of the current Yunmeng County in Hubei) to Jinhua City, Zhejiang Province. Another group moved north from Jiangxia to Liaocheng City (now Gushi in Henan), and then branched out to the south in Anhui, Jiangxi, Fujian and other locations. During the Great Migration of the Great Pagoda Tree of Hongtong in Shanxi in the early years of the Ming Dynasty, the Huangs were among the major migrants and was later relocated in Guangdong, Guangxi, Hunan, Anhui, Jiangsu, Zhejiang, Fujian and other provinces. Today, the population with the surname of Huang is mostly distributed across Guangdong, Fujian, Shandong, Henan, Hebei and other provinces,

洞大槐树的人口大迁移中，黄姓族人是主要的迁民，被分迁至广东、广西、湖南、安徽、江苏、浙江、福建等地。如今，黄姓人口主要分布在广东、福建、山东、河南、河北等地，其中以广东人数为最多。

姓氏起源

黄姓最早出自嬴姓。嬴姓始祖伯益的后裔共有十四支，分别为徐氏、郯氏、莒氏、终黎氏、运奄氏、菟裘氏、将梁氏、黄氏、江氏、修鱼氏、白冥氏、蜚廉氏、秦氏、赵氏等，合称"嬴姓十四氏"。商末周初，黄氏一族在今河南潢川建立了黄国，因被周朝封为子爵，又称"黄子国"。春秋时期，黄子国被楚国吞并。亡国后的黄国子孙因怀念故国，遂以国名为姓，始为黄姓。

黄姓历史名人

黄庭坚（1045—1105），字鲁直，号山谷道人，晚号涪翁，北宋著名诗人、词人、书法家。在诗歌方面，他与北宋文学家、书画家苏轼并称为"苏黄"；在书法方面，与苏轼、米芾、蔡襄并称为"宋代四大家"；在词作方面，与词人秦

among which Guangdong Province has the most Huangs.

Origin of Huang

The surname of Huang originated from the surname of Ying. The first ancestor of the Ying, Bo Yi, had a total of 14 different offspring tribes. They are the so-called 14 Clans of Ying: Xu, Tan, Ju, Zhongli, Yunyan, Tuqiu, Jiangliang, Huang, Jiang, Xiuyu, Baiming, Feilian, Qin and Zhao. During the late Shang Dynasty and early Zhou Dynasty, the Huangs established the State of Huang in what is today's Huangchuan in Henan Province. Since the tribe was dubbed as a viscount (called *Zijue*) in the Zhou Dynasty, the state was also called the State of Huangzi. In the Spring and Autumn Period, the State of Huangzi was taken over by the State of Chu. As a remembrance of the fallen state, descendants of the State of Huangzi took on the state's name as their surname, and thus became the Huangs.

Famous Personages Surnamed Huang in History

Huang Tingjian (1045-1105), courtesy name Luzhi, with the title name of the Taoist of Valley and Senior Fu in his later years, was a famous poet, *Ci* poet and calligrapher in the

● 黄庭坚像
Portrait of Huang Tingjian

观并称为"秦黄"。黄庭坚擅长行书和草书，行书代表作有《黄州寒食诗卷跋》，草书代表作有《李白忆旧游诗卷》。

黄道婆（约1245—约1330），元初著名的棉纺织家。黄道婆出生在松江府乌泥泾镇（今上海徐汇区东湾村）一个贫苦的农民家庭。婚后，她勤于织布、劳作，却遭到夫家的虐待，于是从家乡逃了出来，

Northern Song Dynasty. In the field of poetry, he and Su Shi, a literary writer, calligrapher and painter in the Northern Song Dynasty, were referred to in pair as Su-Huang. In the field of calligraphy, he, along with Su Shi, Mi Fu and Cai Xiang, was collectively known as the Four Masters of the Song Dynasty. In the field of *Ci* poetry, he and Qin Guan, were referred to in pair as Qin-Huang. Huang Tingjian specialized in running and cursive scripts. His representative work in running script is *Postscript to Cold Food Poem in Huangzhou*, and his masterpiece in cursive script is *Cursive-script Poetry Volume of Li Bai Reminiscence of Old Friends*.

Huang Daopo (c.1245-c.1330) was a famous textile and cotton manufacturer during the early Yuan Dynasty. Born into a poor peasant family in Wunijing Town of Songjiang County (now Xuhui District in Shanghai), Huang Daopo began to weave and toil after marriage. However, due to her husband's abuse, she ran away from her hometown, and eventually settled down in Yazhou, Hainan. The local people kindly took her in, and passed their textile techniques on to her. Huang Daopo lived in Hainan for 30 years and mastered such textile

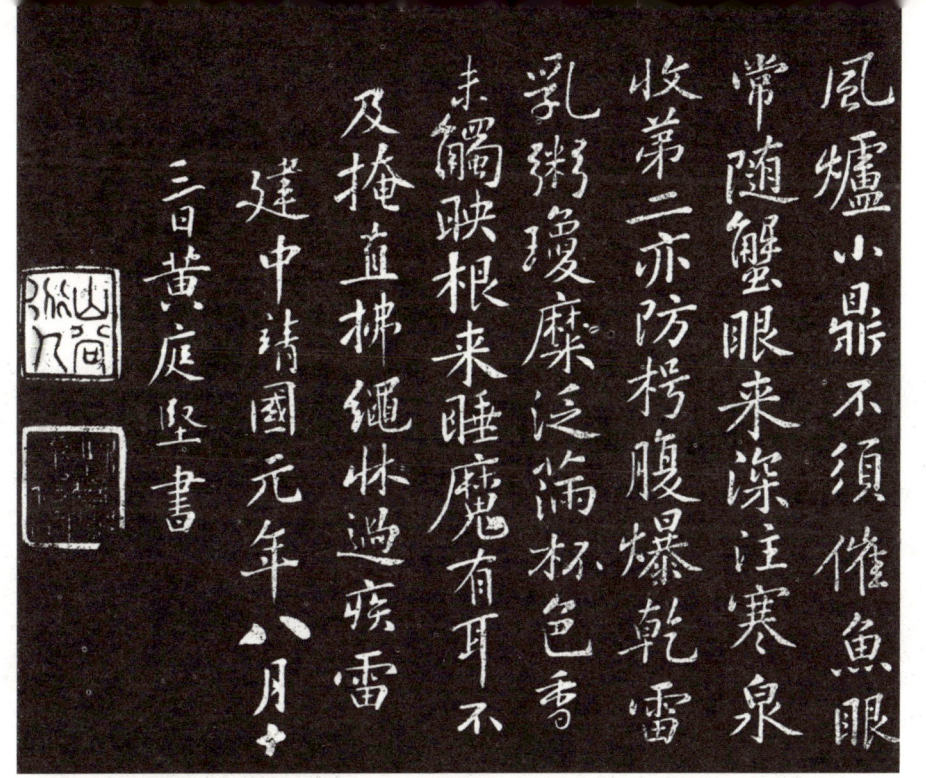

• 《奉同公择尚书咏茶碾煎啜三首》（宋·黄庭坚）
此为黄庭坚的行书作品，题写的字为其诗作，描述了碾茶、煎茶、饮茶等方面的内容。
Three Poems in Ode to Tea, by Huang Tingjian (Song Dynasty, 960-1279)
It was done by Huang Tingjian in running script. The inscribed characters were part of his poems which described the details of grinding, cooking and drinking of tea.

最后在海南崖州落脚。好心的当地居民收留了她，并将当地的纺织技术传授给了她。黄道婆在海南生活了30多年，掌握了捍、弹、纺、织等纺织技术。返回故乡后，她将自己学到的先进的纺织技术传授给了家乡的妇女，还发明了三锭棉纺车，提高了纺棉效率，并总结成一

techniques as guarding, flipping, spinning and weaving. After returning home, Huang Daopo passed her knowledge of the advanced textile techniques on to the local women and invented the three-spindle cotton spinner. She improved the efficiency in cotton spinning and came up with an advanced set of textile techniques which integrated techniques of yarning,

套比较先进的"错纱、配色、综线、挈花"等织造技术。从此,乌泥泾的纺织品名扬天下。

color-matching, lining and pattern-decorating. Since then, textile products of Wunijing became world-renowned items.

- 黄道婆纺纱壁画（图片提供：FOTOE）
Murals of Huang Daopo Spinning Yarn

周姓

目前，周姓人口在中国姓氏中排第九。

早期，周姓族人主要分布在河南、山西等地。魏晋南北朝时期，北方地区政局动荡、战乱不断，周姓族人逐渐南迁至江苏、福建等地。唐宋时期，周姓族人在中国大多数地区都有分布。在明代初年山西洪洞大槐树的人口大迁移中，周姓族人是主要的迁民，被分迁至云南、四川、贵州等地。如今，周姓人口主要分布在湖南、江苏、四川、湖北等地。

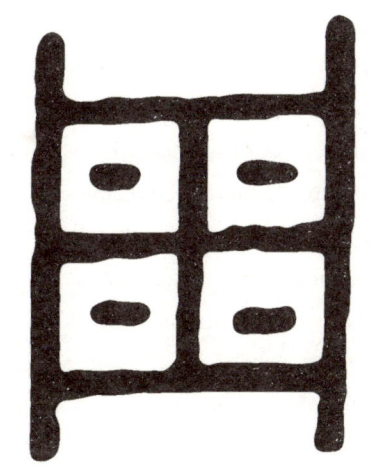

- 甲骨文"周"

Character of *Zhou* in Oracle Bone Script

Zhou

At present, Zhou is ranked ninth among Chinese surnames in terms of population.

In earlier times, the majority of the Zhou clan settled in Henan and Shanxi. During the Wei, Jin, Southern and Northern dynasties, the Zhou clansmen gradually moved south to provinces such as Jiangsu and Fujian due to the ongoing wars and turmoil in the northern regions. By the Tang and Song dynasties, traces of the Zhou family and tribe could be found throughout China. During the Great Migration of the Great Pagoda Tree of Hongtong in Shanxi in the early years of the Ming Dynasty, Zhou was among the major surnames of the migrants and was later relocated in Yunnan, Sichuan, Guizhou and other provinces. Nowadays, the population with the surname of Zhou is mainly distributed across Hunan, Jiangsu, Sichuan and Hubei.

Origin of Zhou

There are two main origins for the surname of Zhou: One is from the surname of Ji, and the other is from the surnames converted from ethnic groups.

Originating from the surname of Ji: Houji, surnamed Ji with the given name Qi, was the ancestor of the Zhou

姓氏起源

周姓的源头主要有两个：一是出自姬姓，二是出自少数民族改姓。

出自姬姓。后稷姓姬，名弃，相传是周王朝的先祖。后稷擅长种植稷、麦等谷物，被尧任用为农师，主管农事。舜统治时期，他因为指导农业生产有功而被赐名后稷。姬发是后稷的后代，于公元前1046年消灭了商朝，建立了周朝，是周朝的开国之君。公元前256年，周朝为诸侯国秦国所灭。周朝王室的后代为了纪念故国，便以"周"为姓。

出自少数民族改姓。南北朝时期，北魏孝文帝大力推行汉化改革，赐予鲜卑族拓跋部落周姓。此后的各个朝代，少数民族与汉族的文化融合，高山族、瑶族、彝族、白族、土家族、黎族、壮族、羌族、朝鲜族等少数民族改姓的汉姓中便有周。

周姓历史名人

周瑜（175—210），字公瑾，是三国时期吴国的著名将领、战略家。西晋时期陈寿编写的史书《三国志》中记载"瑜长壮有姿貌"，

Dynasty in legend. Houji specialized in planting millet, wheat and other grains, and was therefore appointed by Yao as the agricultural officer in charge of farming. During the reign of Shun, he was conferred with the name Houji for his meritorious achievements in guiding agricultural production. Ji Fa, who was the descendant of Houji, eliminated the Shang Dynasty in 1046 B.C. and subsequently established the Zhou Dynasty. In 256 B.C., the Zhou Dynasty was destroyed by the feudal State of Qin. In order to commemorate their fallen country, the imperial descendants of the Zhou Dynasty adopted the name of their state as their surname and became the Zhous.

Originating from the changed surnames of ethnic groups: During the Southern and Northern dynasties, Emperor Xiaowen of the Northern Wei Dynasty vigorously implemented Chinesization and bestowed the Han surname of Zhou upon the Tuoba clan of the Xianbei Tribe. In the following dynasties, ethnic groups, including the Gaoshan, Yao, Yi, Bai, Tujia, Li, Zhuang, Qiang and Korean, adopted Han surnames in the process of interaction and communication with Han people. The surname Zhou was among these Han surnames that were adopted.

称赞他身材高大而威武，样貌俊美。周瑜的军事才能十分突出，最主要的成就便是在赤壁大破曹操的军队。此战之后，魏、蜀、吴三国鼎立的局面形成。除此之外，周瑜还十分擅长音乐，当时有"曲有误，周郎顾"一说。说的是周瑜精通音律，哪怕酒过三巡，如果音乐

• 周瑜像
Portrait of Zhou Yu

Famous Personages Surnamed Zhou in History

Zhou Yu (175-210), courtesy name Gongjin, was a famous general and strategist of the Kingdom of Wu during the Three Kingdoms Period. As recorded in the history book *Romance of the Three Kingdoms* written by Chen Shou during the Western Jin Dynasty (265-317), "Zhou Yu was strong with good-looking appearance"; he was praised for his strong figure and handsome appearance. Zhou Yu's talent in military affairs was so prominent that his most particular achievement was his defeat of Cao Cao's forces in the battle of Red Cliff, which directly determined the tripartite confrontation among the states of Wei, Shu and Wu during the Three Kingdoms Period. In addition to this, Zhou Yu was also well-versed in music. There was a saying that, "Whenever there's a flaw in the song, Zhou Lang would turn a look back." It alluded to Zhou Yu's proficiency in musical temperament that even after the wine was served around three times, Zhou Yu would still be aware of an error in musicality and would take a look back at the performer. In Chinese traditional operas, the role of Zhou Yu is mostly played by young men to display

有误，他亦必然知道，并且回头一顾。在中国传统戏曲中，周瑜多由小生扮演，以表现其儒雅、秀气和英俊。戏曲中的《群英会》《借东风》《三气周瑜》等故事多来自古典名著《三国演义》。

周敦颐（1017—1073），北宋著名哲学家，继承并发展了儒家学说，成为宋明理学的开山鼻祖。理学大家程颢、程颐都是他的学生。其学说在中国思想史上影响深

his refined, elegant and handsome qualities. Plays featuring Zhou Yu, such as *Gathering of Heroes, Harnessing the East Wind, Enraging Zhou Yu Thrice* and many more, are all adapted from the classic *Romance of the Three Kingdoms*.

Zhou Dunyi (1017-1073) was a famous philosopher from the Northern Song Dynasty, who inherited and developed the ideas of Confucian School and became the founder of the Neo-Confucian idealist philosophy. Both Cheng Hao and Cheng Yi, the masterminds of Neo-Confucianism, were his disciples. His theories have exerted far-reaching influence on Chinese philosophy and ideas. Zhou Dunyi's major works were the *All-Embracing Book* and *Explanations of the Tai Chi Diagram*. *Explanations of the Tai Chi Diagram* inherited the ideology of Confucianism and Taoism, and utilized diagrams for the purpose of proposing a system for the theories on the origination of the universe. Zhou Dunyi was also very fond of lotus flowers. He excavated a pool and grew lotuses, calling it the Pond of Lotus Love. He also composed the prose *Ode to the Lotus Flower*, which has been passed down through the ages. In the prose, a metaphor is drawn between Zhou Dunyi

• 周敦颐像
Portrait of Zhou Dunyi

● 莲花
Lotus Flower

远。周敦颐的主要著作是《通书》和《太极图说》。《太极图说》继承了儒家和道教的部分思想，用图形进行推演，提出了宇宙生成论体系。周敦颐还酷爱莲花，曾挖池种莲，并将该池命名为"爱莲池"。他还写作了千古流传的散文《爱莲说》。其中"予独爱莲之出淤泥而不染，濯清涟而不妖，中通外直，不蔓不枝，香远益清，亭亭净植，可远观而不可亵玩焉"之句为周敦颐以出淤泥而不染的莲花自喻，表现了他不与小人同流合污的君子品格。

himself and the lotus flower in such lines as, "I only love the lotus for its purity even though it is grown out of dirty mud, for its cleanness in rippled water without being coquettish, for its unblocked straightforwardness in the inside and unbent posture in the outside, for its being free of entanglements, for its light fragrance even at a distance, and for its decent and simple growth while you can only view in distance rather than hold it in your manipulation." Like the unstained lotus flower, Zhou Dunyi was a man of noble character who never wallowed in the mire with any indecent people.

赤壁之战

　　公元208年，曹操率领军队南下，与孙权、刘备联军在长江流域的赤壁进行了一场大战，史称"赤壁之战"。赤壁之战是中国历史上著名的以少胜多的战役。该战役中，周瑜发挥了他卓越的军事才能。他派部下黄盖诈降曹操。黄盖乘船前往曹操营地，在接近曹营时，以火烧战船，并借助当时猛烈的风势，将火烧至曹营。曹营士兵不谙水性，曹操军队损失惨重。周瑜率领孙、刘五万联军大胜曹操二十万大军，使得曹操的军队实力受损，只能退回长江以北。赤壁之战使得三方实力维持在相对均衡的状态，为形成魏、蜀、吴三分天下的局面奠定了基础。北宋时期著名词人苏轼的《念奴娇·赤壁怀古》便是以赤壁之战为主题的词作。

●《念奴娇·赤壁怀古》

大江东去，浪淘尽，千古风流人物。故垒西边，人道是，三国周郎赤壁。乱石穿空，惊涛拍岸，卷起千堆雪。江山如画，一时多少豪杰！遥想公瑾当年，小乔初嫁了，雄姿英发。羽扇纶巾，谈笑间，樯橹灰飞烟灭。故国神游，多情应笑我，早生华发。人生如梦，一樽还酹江月。

Remembering the Red Cliff, to the Tune of Nian Nu Jiao

The great river flows eastward, sweeping away thousands of generations of gallant heroes in its waves. West of the ancient fort, people say, is the Red Cliff for Zhou Lang of the Three Kingdoms, where rocks stand piercing the sky and shore-tearing waves lash on the bank, rolling up thousand piles of snow. What a picturesque landscape, and how many heroes have gathered at one time! My mind drifts back to those years when Zhou Lang was still young in marriage to the beautiful Qiao. Being vigorous with valor aglow, a feather fan in hand and a silken hat on, he witnessed the ashes of the burnt masts and oars rise and fall over some casual chat. This mere reminiscence of the bygone episode may entitle me as too sentimental and make my hair white. Life is but a dream. Why not pledge this cup of liquor to the river and the moon.

Battle of Red Cliff

In 208, Cao Cao led his army to the south to fight against the allied forces of the state led by Sun Quan and the state led by Liu Bei. A large battle, known in history as the Battle of Red Cliff, thus broke out between both sides at the Red Cliff, located at the Yangtze River Basin. The Battle of Red Cliff was one of the very few famous battles in history of China that the less forces won the final victory. Putting his distinguished military talent into play, Zhou Yu sent his subordinate, Huang Gai, to Cao Cao in false surrender, and ordered him to head toward Cao Cao's camps by boat. Huang Gai was instructed to draw close to Cao's campground and take advantage of the strong wind to sail burning boats to the campground of Cao's army, setting Cao's camps afire. Since Cao's soldiers were not familiar with water-based battles, Cao Cao's army suffered heavy losses. The fifty thousand soldiers from the allied forces of the state of Sun Quan and the state of Liu Bei, led by Zhou Yu, successfully won over Cao Cao's army of two-hundred thousand soldiers, making Cao's army so significantly weakened that Cao Cao had no choice but to retreat back to the north of the Yangtze River. The Battle of Red Cliff established a balance kept among the three sides, making the country divided among the Kingdoms of Wei, Shu and Wu. The famous poem, titled *Remembering the Red Cliff, to the Tune of Nian Nu Jiao* by Su Shi, poet of the Northern Song Dynasty, took the Battle of Red Cliff as its theme.

- 三江口周郎纵火
  小说《三国演义》绣像插画。
  Three-river Estuary where Zhou Yu Set Fires
  Portraits of the illustrations from the novel *Romance of the Three Kingdoms*.

吴姓

目前，吴姓人口在中国姓氏中排第十。

江苏无锡一带是吴姓的发源地，吴姓族人在此繁衍生息。魏晋南北朝时期，吴姓族人大多集中在江苏、浙江、福建等地，呈现出南兴北衰的趋势。唐宋时期，吴姓族人已经遍布中国各地。明清时期，广东、福建沿海的吴姓族人迁移至台湾的人数逐渐增多。如今，吴姓

- 金文"吴"

金文指刻在商周时期青铜器上的铭文，也叫"钟鼎文"。

Character of *Wu* in Bronze Inscription

Bronze inscription refers to the inscription carved on the surfaces of bronze vessels during the Shang and Zhou dynasties. It is also called the Zhong Ding Script (*Zhong* means bell and *Ding* is a sacrificial vessel).

Wu

At present, Wu ranks the tenth among Chinese surnames in terms of population.

The region of Wuxi in Jiangsu Province is the birthplace of the surname Wu. It is from here that the Wu Tribe proliferated and multiplied. During the Wei, Jin, Southern and Northern dynasties, the Wus were mostly concentrated in Jiangsu, Zhejiang and Fujian, displaying a trend of thriving in the south and declining in the north. By the Tang and Song dynasties, the Wus had already spread across China. In the Ming and Qing dynasties, there were growing numbers of Wu tribesmen in the coastal areas of Guangdong and Fujian migrating to Taiwan. Today, the population with the surname of Wu is primarily distributed across Guangxi, Jiangsu, Guizhou, Guangdong and Fujian.

Origin of Wu

There are two main origins for the surname of Wu. One is from the surname of Ji, and the other is from the changed or borrowed surnames of ethnic groups.

Originated from the surname of Ji: Danfu, surnamed Ji, was the leader of the Zhou Tribe in ancient times. Due to the constant intrusions by the northern

人口主要分布在广西、江苏、贵州、广东、福建等地。

姓氏起源

吴姓的源头主要有两个：一是出自姬姓，二是出自少数民族改姓或借姓。

出自姬姓。亶父，姬姓，是上古时期周族的部落首领。由于不断受到北方游牧部落的南下侵扰，亶父带领族人迁往岐山脚下的周原（今陕西岐山县一带）。周族从此在周原定居。亶父生有三子，分别为长子太伯、次子仲雍、三子季历。其中，三子季历最为贤能，具有王者风范。于是他的两个哥哥太伯、仲雍就主动放弃了继承权，离开家乡，一同前往江苏一带，建立了句吴国（即吴国）。公元前473年，吴国灭亡，其后世子孙为了纪念故国，便以国为姓，始为吴姓。

出自少数民族改姓或借姓。少数民族在与汉族融合的发展过程中，改原有少数民族姓氏为汉姓，满族、侗族、壮族、白族等少数民族中便有改姓吴的。还有很多少数民族原本只有名，没有姓，例如苗族，因受到汉族文化

nomadic tribes, Danfu led his tribesmen to Zhouyuan (near the current Qishan County in Shaanxi) at the foot of Qishan Mountain. From then on, the Zhou settled in Zhouyuan. Danfu had three sons, with the eldest son named Taibo, the second son Zhongyong and the youngest son Jili. Among them, Jili was the wisest and most competent, and possessed the majestic demeanor of a ruler. Thus, both his brothers Taibo and Zhongyong voluntarily gave up their rights to the throne, left home and traveled together to the vicinity of Jiangsu Province, where they established the State of Wu. The State of Wu perished in 473 B.C., and to commemorate their lost country, the descendants adopted the name of the state as their surname, Wu.

Originating from the changed or borrowed surnames of ethnic groups: In the process of interaction and communication with Han people, some people from ethnic groups such as the Manchu, Dong, Zhuang and Bai took on Han surnames, and adopted Wu. There were also many ethnic groups, such as the Miao ethnic group, who had only first names but no surnames. Under the influence of Han culture, they adopted Han surnames as their own, and Wu was among these Han surnames.

的影响，借用汉姓，吴便是借用的姓氏之一。

吴姓历史名人

吴道子，唐代著名画家，被后世尊称为"画圣"。吴道子精于佛、道人物画像，擅长壁画创作，代表作品主要有《菩提寺舍利佛》《地狱变相图》《钟馗捉鬼图》《金桥图》等，但其真迹存世者极少，多为后人摹本。吴道子作画不拘成法，喜欢另辟蹊径，师法自然。苏轼在《书吴道子画后》一文

Famous Personages Surnamed Wu in History

Wu Daozi, a famous painter from the Tang Dynasty, was respectfully called the Sage of Painting by later generations. He was well-versed in Buddha and Taoist portraits and murals. Some of his representative works include *Shariputra at the Bodhi Temple, Transformation of the Hell, Zhong Kui Catching Ghosts* and *The Golden Bridge.* However, very few of his original works have survived. Most existing works are copies made by people in later generations. Wu Daozi was not confined to routine methods but enjoyed finding new means and styles, being inspired by nature. In *Epilogue to Wu Daozi's Painting*, Su Shi wrote, "Poetry culminated in Du Zimei, prose in Han Tuizhi, calligraphy in Yan Lugong, and painting in Wu Daozi. Everything good and changeable has been ended by these people!" This line expresses the idea that Du Fu, Han Yu, Yan Zhenqing and Wu Daozi established the benchmark for poetry, prose, calligraphy and painting culminated in. This is a statement in high

• 吴道子像
Portrait of Wu Daozi

- 《维摩诘像》
  此壁画位于敦煌103窟东壁南侧，被认为具有吴道子的画风。

  Portrait of Vimalakirti
  The mural is located on the south side of the east wall in Cave No. 103 of Dunhuang, is considered to have Wu Daozi's artistic style.

中写道："诗至于杜子美，文至于韩退之，书至于颜鲁公，画至于吴道子，而古今之变，天下之能事毕矣"。意思是，诗歌到了杜甫，散文到了韩愈，书法到了颜真卿，绘画到了吴道子，这几门文学、艺术的成就，已经是通古今之变化，达到登峰造极的境界了。

吴承恩（约1500—1583），明代著名小说家，中国古典名著《西游记》的作者。《西游记》以唐代玄奘法师西行印度求取佛经的经历为故事原型，讲述了唐僧、孙悟空、猪八戒、沙僧师徒四人到西天取经，在途中历经九九八十一难后终于修成正果的故事。作者借助

praise of the achievements made by these individuals.

Wu Cheng'en (c. 1500-1583), was a famous novelist in the Ming Dynasty and authored the Chinese classic *Journey to the West*. *Journey to the West* is based on the story of Xuanzang, a Buddhist master in the Tang Dynasty, in his westbound trip to India to obtain Buddhist scriptures. The novel tells of Xuanzang and his three apprentices, Sun Wukong (the Monkey King), Zhu Bajie (the Pig) and Sha Wujing (the Monk), as they headed to the West, went through 81 trials on the way, and ultimately succeeded in attaining the ultimate result. The author utilized the mythical characters in *Journey to the West* to express his dissatisfaction and anger in

《西游记》中的人物抒发了对现实的不满和对封建科举制度的愤懑,以及改变现实的愿望。《西游记》已经被翻译成日、英、法、德、俄等十几种文字。《美国大百科全书》评价《西游记》是"一部具有丰富内容和光辉思想的神话小说"。《法国大百科全书》也认为"全书故事的描写充满幽默和风趣,给读者以浓厚的兴味"。

protest against the harsh reality and the feudal system of imperial examinations, as well as his desire to change the reality. *Journey to the West* has been translated into more than 10 different languages, including Japanese, English, French, German and Russian. *Encyclopedia American* praises *Journey to the West* as a mythic novel with rich content and brilliant ideas, and the *French Encyclopedia* highlights the humor and wit in the book.

● 吴承恩像(图片提供:FOTOE)
Portrait of Wu Cheng'en

复姓
Compound Surnames

复姓指字数为两个或两个以上的姓氏，是中国姓氏的重要组成部分。复姓的来源主要有以下几种：一是以官职为姓，例如上官、司马；二是以封地为姓，例如欧阳；三是少数民族姓氏或改姓，例如爱新觉罗、尉迟。

Compound surnames refer to surnames consisting of two or more characters. They are an important part of Chinese surnames. There are three primary origins of compound surnames. The first is from the name of official, such as Shangguan and Sima; the second is from the name of the manor conferred, such as Ouyang; and the third is from the surnames or changed surnames of ethnic groups, such as Aisin Gioro and Yuchi.

上官

芈姓是古楚人的姓氏。战国时期，楚怀王赐封他的儿子芈子兰为上官大夫（古代官职名）。子兰的后世子孙便以官职为姓，始姓上官。

Shangguan

The surname Mi is a surname of the ancient people in Chu. During the Warring States Period, King Huai of Chu conferred the position of Shangguan minister upon his son Mi Zilan. Zilan's offspring adopted the name of the official as their surname.

司马

司马是商代时开始设立的官职，与司徒、司空、司士、司寇并称"五官"，共同掌管军政、军赋等。司马作为姓氏，起源于西周时期，不同的分支有不同的始祖，但都以司马这一官职为姓：一是周宣王时期（前827—前782）的司马程伯休父，二是春秋时期楚国的司马芈子反，三是春秋时期晋国的司马韩厥。

Sima

Sima was an official position established in the Shang Dynasty, together with the official positions Situ, Sikong, Sishi and Sikou, constituted of five officials jointly in charge of military administrations and military taxes. As a surname, Sima originated from the Western Zhou Dynasty, and its different branch clans came from ancestors of different surnames, all of which took on the name of this official position as their surname. One such ancestor was the Sima by the name of Chengbo Xiufu from the King Xuan of Zhou Period (827 B.C.-782 B.C.). The second source was the Sima by the name of Mi Zifan of the State Chu from the Spring and Autumn Period. The third was the Sima by the name of Han Jue of the State Jin from the Spring and Autumn Period.

欧阳

夏朝时，帝王少康封其子无余于会稽（今浙江绍兴）。无余在会稽建立了越国，公元前306年，越国为楚国所灭。越王无疆的次子被赐封到欧余山的南部，因古人以山南为阳，便称他"欧阳亭侯"。其后世子孙以封地为姓，始姓欧阳。

Ouyang

During the Xia Dynasty, Emperor Shaokang assigned his son, Wu Yu, to the manor estate of Kuaiji (now Shaoxing in Zhejiang Province). Wu Yu established the State of Yue in Kuaiji, which was later destroyed by the State of Chu in 306 B.C. The second son of Wu Jiang, the King of Yue, was assigned to the southern region of Ouyu Mountain. Since ancient people called the south side of mountains as *Yang*, the second son of Wu Jiang was therefore referred to as the Precinct Marquis of Ouyang. His descendants thereafter adopted this as their surname, and thus began the surname of Ouyang.

司马迁像

司马迁，西汉时期著名史学家、文学家。他编撰了中国第一部纪传体通史《史记》。

Portrait of Sima Qian

Sima Qian was a famous historian and writer in the Western Han Dynasty, who compiled China's first biographical general history, the *Historical Records*.